Starkey's Boys

The U.S. Salvage Navy and Navy Deep Sea Diving in the Hawaiian Islands

by

Christopher P. LaVoie

Bloomington, IN Milton Keynes, UK

authorHOUSE

AuthorHouse™
1663 Liberty Drive, Suite 200
Bloomington, IN 47403
www.authorhouse.com
Phone: 1-800-839-8640

AuthorHouse™ UK Ltd.
500 Avebury Boulevard
Central Milton Keynes, MK9 2BE
www.authorhouse.co.uk
Phone: 08001974150

First published by AuthorHouse 3/28/2006

ISBN: 1-4259-1993-6 (sc)

Library of Congress Control Number: 2006902309

Printed in the United States of America
Bloomington, Indiana

This book is printed on acid-free paper.

Contents

I floated effortlessly at a depth of around forty feet, four stories below the surface, in the cool and cloudy harbor water of Pearl Harbor Naval Base in Hawaii. The message coming to me from the diving supervisor above was that I had missed the ship's propeller, or screw, by a few yards and I needed to move in a new direction. I stopped and peered through the waters, searching for the vessel's screw. It was early morning with the only light coming from flood lights set up on the pier next to our dive station. A slight shadow caught my eye and I started for it.

My bright yellow umbilical cord that carried my air and communication cables drifted along behind me. I kept one hand on it to prevent any entanglement. My face mask was the new full face rig, commonly called the AGA rig, that allowed me to move as if I were in SCUBA mode, but gave me direct voice communications with the dive supervisor above. I pumped my stiff, black rubber, military issue fins to send me and the fifty odd feet of umbilical towards what I had seen.

The ship's screw, almost twelve feet in diameter, slowly came into focus through the murky harbor waters. I found myself dwarfed by the huge, steel prop before me. I held onto the center, where the ship's port side shaft held the screw and connected it to the main engines and reduction gear. All the internal engineering machinery was supposed to have been shut down before my dive. One diver from our team would have been sent to double check this prior to putting divers in the water. If they missed even one pump or suction intake valve, it could be a fast death for a navy diver passing over the seawater intake port on the ships hull.

I could still hear some unknown machinery operating. The sound could have been traveling from another ship in the harbor as sound travels well under water. I had to trust that the ship I was working on was secure. Trust was the bond that held the diving navy together. Without it, people can get hurt or die in this business.

I announced to the diving supervisor that I was at the screw. The supervisor advised me, his voice crackling through the dive rig's comms, breaking in and out, that a second diver was on the way. With him will be a heavy steel braided cable to attach to the vessel's screw. The idea was to take the weight of the screw off the vessel's main shaft after my dive buddy and I disconnected the lock nuts holding it. The damaged screw could then be slid off the shaft and raised out of the water.

This was not a dive operation that was attempted regularly, but this was no regular time. It was the heart of the first gulf war and we were working on an Aegis equipped, Ticonderoga class, guided missile cruiser. The ship was expected in the gulf waters off the coast of Kuwait in a short time and the captain had no intention of being late. The Pacific Command Admiral had no intention of listening to excuses either. The requests from Pearl Harbor officials to dry dock the cruiser for a safer removal of the screw were denied. At one in the morning, the commanding officer of the Pearl Harbor dive locker was called and told to get a team of divers on station as soon as possible.

A few hours later, there I was, forty feet below the harbor's surface staring at a multi-ton screw and trying to understand just how the hell I was going to pull this operation off. I understood the basic idea of it all; secure the cable to the screw and remove the huge nuts and other locking devices that kept it on the shaft. After that we were to guide this damn thing back to the surface. This dive was an unconventional and emergency job so the diving supervisor was Master Diver Ed Starkey himself. Starkey, with a sausage sized finger sticking in my face, gave me one word of advice before I geared up; "screw this job up La'hoy'a and you'll be hobbling to the base hospital to have my boot removed from your butt!" Words of encouragement, at three am when the whole dive team was either hung over or still drunk, were in order, I guess.

I waited for my second diver to arrive with the heavy cable. Blue diver, as he was designated, to keep him from being confused with my 'red' designation, followed my umbilical down to me with a line in tow. Together we heaved around on the line to bring the steel braided cable down and over to our site. With blue diver was a wrench device I had never seen before. Master Diver Starkey's gruff and loud voice, again crackling in and out on slightly salt water-shorted comm lines, explained that it was part of a larger piece of gear that would remove the lock nuts and securing bolts from the ship's shaft and screw. I had no idea how it worked and it came with no instructions. Business as usual in the dive navy.

Blue diver and I worked the bizarre wrench and attached gear to remove the oversized nut and locking mechanisms from the shaft. Instead of the bolts turning, the device succeeded in spinning the two of us into the ships hull at full speed, slamming us hard into the steel. Master Diver Starkey heard the noise over the comms and the dull 'thud' sound on the ship's hull. Starkey called down to red and blue diver for an explanation. I was holding my right side in pain and blue diver was shaking his head, trying to clear the dazed effect by the impact. Neither of us wanted to piss off the Master Diver and it would not have meant holding up the job anyhow, so we reported that we were fine and just learning how to operate the heavy wrench device they had lowered down to us.

The Master Diver radioed down to us over the comm lines "don't break the damn shaft, you two screw-ups, or I'll have your heads on a stake!" The method was rough, but the point was clear. The Pacific Command expected a guided missile cruiser in the gulf on time regardless of how many high school educated, half drunk divers had to die to get it there. Point taken. It was alright coming from Master Diver Starkey though, he had been putting his life on the line for some admiral's damn schedule for over thirty years now. He had been in my shoes only too many times before.

We tied heavy lines to the shaft bolts as they were removed and guided them to the surface. We then kicked our fins to take us to the top of one of the screws blades. The top blade, or blade 'one', did not always mean the one facing up. It was the one with a steel plug in it that could be removed to place a heavy eye bolt inside for lifting off the screw. Remember, this was all supposed to happen in the controlled and 'safety first' environment of a dry dock facility. As it turned out for my dive buddy and I, the top blade was far over to the starboard side. It would have to be spun around by the lifting cable slowly before the screw could be removed from the shaft.

The cool waters of Pearl Harbor in the morning hours chilled me right through the full wet suit I was wearing. I shivered as I breathed and my hands were shaking involuntarily as I worked the eye bolt into the hole provided for it on the 'top' blade. It took several turns to get it fully seated, blue diver had the eye bolt on a line just in case I lost hold of it. If we lost that damn thing in the mud about twenty feet below us we may as well slit our own throats with our stainless steel dive knives as that was just what Master Diver Starkey was going to do anyhow.

Shivering, I announced to the dive station that the eye bolt was in. Blue diver handed me the line to help heave around on the heavy steel cable that drifted about ten feet from us just behind the ship's screw. On the end of the cable was a ready fitted 'U' shaped salvage shackle. A shackle is a seventy to one hundred pound steel bolt that is used to secure two very heavy objects together in both above and under water environments. The shackle worked easy enough, but was usually the weakest point in the chain created. The idea was to secure the damn thing and get out of the way.

Blue diver and I worked with shaking hands and bruised bodies to attach the heavy shackle to the eye bolt on the screw's blade. One man turned the attachment bolt while the other held the diver to the blade to keep him from spinning instead of the bolt and wrench. Working underwater was much like working in space. Do not expect that when a diver pushes something it is going to move. More than likely the diver is going to go backwards and, unlike in space, underwater they had better know what was behind them.

For about ten solid minutes I worked my arms hard to turn the shackle bolt around. I was bleeding from my hands and arms where I had hit the hull and screw, cutting myself on various jagged shards of steel. I even bled from my scalp just above the full face dive mask I was wearing. Blue diver had to point that one out to me. I was in so much pain I did not even notice.

Once secured, blue diver and I kicked our fins to get us about five feet from the screw and about five feet below the eye bolt. If it was going to break and send that steel braided cable flying, I wanted to be below it. I called to Master Diver Starkey to heave around slow on the lifting cable so as to bring the blade with the eye bolt up from the starboard angle to the top. I looked over at blue diver next to me and gave him a shivering thumbs up. He was holding his body with his arms to conserve heat and gave me a nod.

The massive mobile crane the Master Diver had called in from the far side of the naval base was stationed just above the dive site and even forty feet below water I could hear the heavy engines turning over and revving up the RPMs. The Master Diver called down to ask where we were and I told him we were below the eye bolt and about three meters off the screw.

With a loud revving of the crane's engines the steel braided cable began to take up slack and put a strain on the screw's main blade. The cruiser's screw, several tons in weight and sitting solid on the main shaft, made a loud cranking noise and jerked counter clockwise a few inches. The noise carried like a physical force underwater and hit blue diver's and my ears loud enough to hurt. We made a futile gesture to cover our ears even though we knew that underwater the sound would still travel right through our bodies and into our inner ear as if we had not even bothered to try to stop it.

The crane's engines revved again, muffled by the harbor water, and took another strain on the steel cable. The screw gave another loud metal on metal grinding noise and shifted counter clockwise with a quick jerking motion. I thought fast to myself; "this is not good." The sudden motion of the screw turning had broken free any hold friction had in keeping the propeller onto the shaft. Under the pendulum effect of the steel lifting cable, the screw slid off of the cruiser's main shaft and came swinging right for me with all its weight and at dangerous speed.

Blue diver and I kicked our fins in front of us violently to get out of the way, but it was too late. The huge, heavy tonnage ship's screw slammed into me sending me backwards fast and reeling in pain as if I had been struck by a Mack truck. My AGA dive mask was ripped from my face and all the air was forced out of my lungs. My umbilical, attached to my waist with a 'D' ring, wrapped around one of the screw's blades. Before I could get my bearings and still feeling the lightning bolt of pain searing through my body from head to legs, the cruiser's screw pendulum-swung back towards the shaft taking my umbilical, and me, with it.

I was jerked towards the ship with a whip like speed and I felt myself being drug through the water behind the screw. With a loud 'Gong' sound the screw slammed back into the shaft, slightly off angle which sent it into a spin motion as it dangled from the steel cable. One of the spinning blades struck me like a batter swinging a baseball bat. I was sent into another direction until my umbilical, tangled around the screw, went tight and snapped back on me like a bull whip.

Master Diver Starkey was screaming into the comms for some answers to all the loud noises and jerks on the umbilical cords. Blue diver came kicking his fins towards me as I dangled from the screw like a puppet on a string. With one hand I was searching for my face mask, found it, and put it back up to my face to breathe. Blue diver pulled the rubber head straps that held the mask onto my face over my hair and behind my head. Meanwhile I could hear him calling up to dive station saying that everything was under control and that we needed a minute to position the screw for its ascent to the surface. Half of navy diving was convincing the supervisor that a diver knew what they were doing. If a diver has to call for help, and the dive supervisor has to deploy that third 'safety' diver sitting on the pier, someone had better be missing a limb down there.

The AGA mask was full of water so I instinctively pressed the purge button to clear it. I was still dazed and in pain so I forgot to hold the mask off of my face as I cleared it and succeeded in forcing a pint of water and high pressure air into my lungs and stomach. I coughed violently and spat up some water from my throat. After a second or two I was breathing again and with blue diver's help I cleared my umbilical from the screw.

Together blue diver and I inspected the cruiser's shaft for damage, it was thankfully light and would not impede the screw replacement. We looked at each other and shook our heads at how close we came to getting our necks broke...by Starkey, not the screw. I kicked my fins, through intense physical pain, to get the screw positioned for the crane to lift it away.

Coughing and breathing heavy, I told dive station to take up the cable. Blue diver and I kicked our fins hard and heaved around on the guide line attached to the screw to keep it steady as it was lifted. The crane on the pier next to the cruiser was revving hard to get enough pull on the cable. A minute or two went by as we guided the screw out of the water and into the waiting hands of several harbor workers. They took the guide lines from us and eased the screw onto the back of a huge flatbed trailer attached to a dark gray semi truck. It was over.

The dive station personnel assisted blue diver and I out of the water and began to gear up two new divers for the next phase of the dive operation. It was now just beginning to break daylight and the flood lamps set up on dive station to give us some visibility under water were turned off. Master Diver Starkey chewed my ass off for a solid fifteen minutes about how an officer from the cruiser had called down to them asking what had hit the ship and if there was any damage.

I stood there, wet, cold, tired and in pain from head to toe and just nodded my head as Starkey's every word tore through me. "Damn-it La'hoy'a, everyone but the admiral himself was asking me questions about the noises! What the hell do you think we are running here? I sent you to do a damn job and you ..." My weary eyes drifted away from the Master Diver's face.

Over Master Diver Starkey's shoulder I could see the young dive officer from our command that had been assigned to 'supervise' the screw removal operation. The cruiser's captain, the dive officer and a third officer, probably from Pearl Harbor Command, were shaking hands and smiling. They were congratulating the dive officer on a job well done and telling him how competent his leadership was in this successful operation. I just shook my head and smiled. My gaze drifted back to Starkey's face, now red, sweaty and about two inches from mine.

"Oh...you think this is funny? A damn joke to smile about La'hoy'a? I'll shove my foot so far up your butt...!"

Chapter 1

Orders to paradise.

Great lakes, Illinois in January is very cold. In fact, to call the United States Naval training center in Great Lakes, Illinois cold is a serious understatement. The temperature is arctic before wind chill is figured in. Close to Lake Michigan and about one hour by train from Chicago, Great Lakes was the most bone freezing, isolated and depressing Naval installation a poor young sailor could be stationed at.

Less than one year into my naval enlistment, I tried to picture the adventurous and adrenaline pumped recruitment posters that brought me here. I may have signed up to be a navy diver, but I had to get through six months in this place to make that happen.

I stood at 0630 hours outside the red brick barracks building that I called home. With me stood about two hundred other new, young sailors waiting for morning colors to sound so we could be marched off to breakfast and school. The wind and cold froze me right through the many layers of my military cold weather uniform I wore. I shivered and felt the moisture on my lips freeze. The dark blue Navy wool coat I wore flapped against the morning winds. Every time the collar blew up and hit my face it stung like a full fisted punch on my ice chilled skin.

Great Lakes Naval base was primarily designed for the engineering training that sailors received after boot camp. Great lakes was manned by both civilian instructors and military supervisors. The educational programs given to new sailors sent here were electronics, welding, engine maintenance and the navy gunners mate programs. Gunners mates were small weapons operators and repairmen. They also worked on the navy's phalanx anti missile defense systems. If a sailor was training in Great Lakes, they were not going

1

into an administrative or "admin" position. They were going to earn their pay the hard way.

The layout of Great Lakes had not been changed since world war two. The buildings were red brick with wood framed windows. The roads were paved but the snow and ice made them a filthy, frozen mud mess. Various unidentifiable antennae protruded from the training buildings. Power cables and telephone lines zig zagged around the base like an icicle strewn web of confusion. That is just what I felt Great Lakes projected. Confusion.

As morning colors sounded over the base speaker system, a traditional tune used in the United States military, my group of students and I were ordered to attention. After the flags were raised, I was marched in line to breakfast. Great Lakes had the worlds largest military mess hall. The size of a stadium, it had at least a half dozen different chow lines allowing thousands of sailors to filter in and out all day. Each meal served to this base could feed a decent sized town. Great Lakes was massive.

At breakfast, I filled my thermos with hot coffee and made my way to the Electrical Engineering school. I officially entered the Navy to be a Deep Sea Diver, but all divers had to go through an engineering rate (school) of some sort. My rate was EM or electricians mate. Basically I worked with generators and motors. The joke was that anything that needed a cord or cable to run it was an EM's responsibility.

The pictures I remembered from the recruiter's office, divers working in their shorts and t-shirts welding and bolting ships together, did not fit the life I was living in Great Lakes; this frozen and muddy wasteland with thousands of long faced men and snow covered cars. What was this life? How did I end up here from my warm and wonderful basic training in Orlando Florida? Talk about a drastic change in climates!

Drastic changes were not unusual to me. My father was a United States Marine and we moved from base to base every two years. I had lived in many different climates, states and cities. It was interesting to now be in the military myself and moving around so much. I guess all "military brats", children of soldiers and sailors, are basically gypsies at heart. It goes with the territory. The first chance I had to settle down, I go and join the Navy, "see the world...adventure", and all of that.

Here I was in Great Lakes EM school with thousands of strangers. Another point about being a military brat is that I learned to make friends fast. I had to. It is almost a survival instinct. My life was moving from base to base around the country. When I would arrive at a new base, I would look out the window and see kids playing basketball together on the base court. I could either stay inside and become a depressed recluse or go out and meet them. By now in life I had no trouble just walking up to people and saying hello. I made friends at Great Lakes without trouble and there were about twenty other diver wanna-bees on the base with me. I identified them quickly and our group stuck together.

Electrical Engineering school was great for a gear and tech nut like me. I enjoyed learning about elevator repair and basic wiring. EM seemed like a rate I could get used to. EM's tended to be somewhat nerdy, but we had common sense. That's how they discerned between ET's and EM's. ET's, or electronic technicians, were the real deal geeks in the navy. Geniuses yes, common sense, well, god bless them anyhow, they got good jobs when their navy career ended, so I guess it all evens out.

EM's were basically ET's who drank too much. EM's could not be trusted with the high tech stuff. So the navy had EM's re-wiring magnetic motors and generators the size of Volkswagens instead. I guess the navy figured EM's could not break much there. EM was my rate and I fit right in. Stand on the rubber mat, pass out the electricians gloves, make sure my next of kin file is updated and get to work.

Great Lakes had one women's barracks in the center of the base. Most female sailors did not care for the engineering rates so they went off to sunny and warm training bases around the United States to study. Those who could handle it, and these gals could, went to Great Lakes like the rest of the poor bastards.

The female barracks had various nicknames. Most are not fit to print I assure you. The female barracks buildings themselves were built like Fort Knox. Why not, they protected the gold all the young male sailors on base wanted to get at. Flood lights, fences, walls of stone and security cameras protected the female barracks from all angles. A far cry from the other barracks on base. Heck, the barracks I lived in often did not have running water, let alone hot. Lets just say the female barracks were an oasis of sanity in the center of nuts-ville.

On my way to training every morning I walked past the female barracks. A few dozen sailors were always hanging out in the general area of the women's barracks. Waiting for, well, I am not really sure. No matter what the weather though, they were there.

I realized something about the military staff at Great Lakes that I found very interesting. Every naval staff member, training instructors, barracks supervisors and all the way up to the officers who watched over the various schools themselves, were there because they had screwed up in their career somewhere. Every Great Lakes instructor had a story behind how they got transferred from the ships and bases of the world to Great-freaking-Lakes, Illinois. Each instructor, in their own way, pissed off the wrong person. For what ever reason, here they were. Great Lakes was the end of the road as far as a navy career went.

We were in this together. Instructors, sailors, everyone. All stuck in Great Lakes, in the middle of winter. In Great Lakes, depression was fought off with cheap beer, bad pizza and good pornography. The best advice was to layer your clothes and write home often because no one is leaving anytime soon.

I arrived at the Electricians school and checked my inbox. I had a note inside. An appointment slip.

The slip of paper read that I had an appointment to get a dental exam at the Great Lakes naval hospital. The Great Lakes naval hospital was located on the far side of base over a bridge and, I am not making this up, through the woods. It was another world engineering school students only heard about, but dared not believe in. Stories of the hospital made their way around base in the hush of night. Sailors dreamed of this place, but were not allowed to enter it.

You think I am kidding here. The naval hospital actually had security to keep the engineering school peasants out. A sailor needed an official doctor's appointment to get into the place. One of the reasons for this level of security was the school located on the hospital grounds; Naval Corpsmen school. Allow me to explain.

Corpsmen were the navy enlisted medical personnel. These were the good looking men and women of the navy who actually did well in high school. Corpsmen were enlisted but lived like officers. Male Corpsmen were all tall and lean and the women were all beautiful and built. The Great Lakes naval hospital was a mythical place a sailor was willing to self inflict an injury to get into. The hospital was a place of positive energy. Clean white buildings and, god help me, trees. Real, green, living bushes and trees.

Today I held the golden pass. The doctors appointment slip. The paper was signed by the EM school officer in charge and all. It was legitimate. A passport to the real world just beyond the fence line that kept the heathens at bay in the engineering training center. I walked towards the fence line gate and the security check point that separated the engineering school and the hospital grounds. I could not actually see the hospital from the engineering side, but I knew it was there, hiding.

As I made my way closer to the security gate building, an armed guard readied himself. The guard had no doubt seen this before. Half crazed, half drunk and sex starved engineering school sailors charging the gates to the

Great Lakes naval hospital like French peasants storming the Bastille! The guard widened his stance and held up his rifle to resist the onslaught.

"I have an appointment." I exclaimed, holding the note up high and proud. A ray of sunlight beamed down from the cloudy, engineering school's side sky. Its beam of light shown directly onto the paper slip I held in the air illuminating it like a golden relic. "Dental exam."

"Oh…O.K." The guard sighed in relief and relaxed his stance. He stood back inside the guard shack and I walked through the gates. Out of the wasteland and into the real world.

I could feel a sort of weight come off my shoulder as I crossed into the Naval Hospital side of base. I walked through the woodland and made my way towards the medical facility. Even the air seemed cleaner on this side of the gate.

As I wandered closer to the tall white buildings of the naval hospital, I looked over the trees, clean cars and shoveled sidewalks. This is what a naval base in the winter should look like. Various groups of sharp dressed medical students walked along the sidewalks and roadways. The corpsmen talked cheerfully and carried medical texts. Their hair was well groomed and they all looked as if they took aerobics classes. No one was sloppy or dishelmed. The corpsmen students, of course, noticed me a mile away.

The medical students would see me and get quiet. They would whisper to themselves "look…it is one of them…from, you know…over there." It was humorous enough to actually make me laugh out loud a few times; no doubt adding to my already poor presentation before the hospital students and staff. Not only was I the only one on base wearing wrinkled blue navy dungarees instead of crisp dress uniforms, but I was laughing like a deranged madman every time I crossed a group of med school students. I was lucky they didn't whisk me from the open and lock me away for observation before I could infect the whole base with my sloth-ness.

The halls of the hospital buildings were clean and white. Loudspeakers notified various doctors of their calls and meetings. Beautiful nurses carried documents and medical gear to and fro. Paintings in well matched frames hung from the walls and the furniture looked new. What a change this was. The barracks I lived in had plaster peeling from the walls and the furniture was so beat up I figured it was confiscated from Germany after WWII. The temperature in the hospital was perfect and warm. I did not feel sweaty or chilled, mind you, that would be imperfect. That is what the naval hospital was…perfect.

At the Dental office the young, attractive nurse working the front desk did not even look me in the eye as she handed me a clipboard and rattled off a thirty second monologue she had memorized. I filled out the history forms and returned them. Again without a look, the nurse instructed me to return to my seat until called. She even told me that the water fountain and restrooms were down the hall to the right. No doubt she had endured countless attempts by engineering school heathens to hit on her with such petty questions and figured to just bypass the opportunity for me. Hell, it worked.

I took my seat in the waiting lounge. A color television on mute flickered from one corner of the room. Magazines and navy news bulletins were neatly stacked on the end table. I looked around and just took it all in. I could have slept on these seats. The furniture at the hospital had cushions thicker than the ex-U-boat mattresses my barracks used.

I looked down the hall towards another medical department. I could see another engineering school student seated in its waiting area. He was easy to spot with his un-kept blue work uniform and scuffed black boots. He too was looking at the walls and floors of the hospital in wonder. The image made me laugh again out loud. Hearing me, the nurse glanced up from her paperwork and frowned. I guess the peasants were not expected to speak unless spoken to around here. Screw her.

After my dental exam I decided to soak my pass for all it was worth and have lunch in the hospital cafeteria. The hospital did not have a mess hall, it had a "cafeteria." Get it? Good.

The cafeteria was clean and neat. The food was recognizable and delicious. A television broadcasted news and other shows at the far end of the room. Everyone sat and chatted as they ate. There were groups of well dressed and well groomed medical students. In the middle of the room, alone on a table, enduring whispers and side glances from all around me, I sat.

I savored every bite of my lunch. Real food, hot, fresh. I bet myself that nothing I was eating was packaged during the Vietnam war or needed water to re-hydrate. This was actual food. I ate until I could eat no more. As I walked out I filled another cola from the cafeteria's dispenser. The hospital cafeteria had soda and soft serve ice cream on demand. It was another world, man.

With reluctance, I began my walk back to the engineering school side. As I retraced my steps towards the guard shack, I felt the real world slowly disappear. The closer I got to the engineering school side, the more I noticed clouds gathering again. The snow became dirtier. The trees looked worse and sick until ultimately there were no more. I was leaving this place of dreams.

I turned my head to catch a last look at the glistening white tops of the hospital buildings. The chatter of med school students now gone as the mud and wind took their place. I waved a slow and reluctant hand at the gate guard as I passed through. He watched me go through and gave me a nod. The guard knew what I felt. Here he sat all day; at the gates of purgatory. One side was heaven and the other, well, home.

Once back inside the engineering school base I stopped to allow a big, old, gray school bus to pass full of trainees. As it passed it showered me with muddy wet slush from the street. I looked down at myself covered in dirt and filth. My face was dripping mud and sand. I laughed out loud and didn't care who heard me. I was an engineering rate sailor, by god.

Engineers made the ships go and kept them running in a time of war. Engineers were not expected to be clean or polite. We did not wear ironed, crisp uniforms or shiny polished shoes. Engineers wore dirty blue dungarees, black boots and ball caps.

The officers and gentler-rates may look down on engineering sailors here, in this god forsaken miserable training center, but on the seas, when the ship has taken two missiles in its side and the fires are spreading through their precious "cafeteria", the more "refined" crew members will cry like children for their mothers hoping the damage control engineers will come up from the bowels of the ship's engine spaces to save their asses.

Engineers fight the fires, repair the damage, save the ship and others get the medals for it. Absolutely god damn right. I wouldn't have it any other way.

I walked back towards EM school. I had a long day ahead of me with school and studies. I was proud.

When the training day ended, I met with the other diver-hopefuls in the base gym. The Great Lakes gym was well built and full of training equipment. Every day the men who were part of the navy's dive program met to work out together and keep themselves motivated. Each diver candidate at engineering school knew that after training in Great Lakes was completed they would be split up to the various dive schools around the nation. The SEAL, Sea Air Land, hopefuls would go to San Diego, California. The EOD, Explosive Ordinance Disposal, hopefuls would go to a U.S. Air Force base to begin training with candidates from various military branches. Those who were going to Deep Sea school would divide to either Panama City, Florida or Pearl Harbor, Hawaii.

Right now divers just had to get through the basic rate training. If divers failed here, no dive school. For this reason candidates kept each other motivated. On cold and windy afternoons, when most of the base emptied into the bars and malls nearby, the dive program boys changed into their work out gear.

One dive candidate, Gordon, was in EM school with me and we quickly became friends. We worked out after each day of training and studied for tests together. Gordon was from California and grew up in a very different world from my mostly mid-western background. The Navy was like that. People who never would have known each other become friends for life.

Gordon's father was a hard working electrician and he worked with him during summer breaks. No doubt, the EM field was attractive to him as he already had some knowledge of electrical work. Frozen Great Lakes was a big change for Gordon from the warm days of California.

Gordon and I knew how important it was to stay in shape while finishing our initial engineering training. If we arrived at dive school out of shape we would not make it through. Six months in Great Lakes could make or break the physical condition of a dive candidate. If the other divers wanted to cancel exercise and head out on the town instead, Gordon and I would stay focused and hit the base gym.

When all the dive candidates got together to work out they changed the program now and then to keep the afternoon from getting monotonous. Often the dive candidates took their gym time to the outdoor field. Frozen and covered with snow, they would carry a stone hard frozen telephone pole around the running track. The pole would weigh a ton with the water frozen into it.

Yelling and singing boot camp marching cadence, myself and the rest of the dive hopefuls would walk laps with that damn pole. From the warmth of the barracks and training buildings faces would peer out of windows to watch the group. The other Great Lakes students would shake their heads and make comments at our lack of sanity. Perhaps they were right. No one in their right mind would be out in the below zero wind of a Great Lakes, Illinois afternoon carrying a frozen pole around a snow covered running track. No one but us.

After the work out I painfully walked back to the barracks to shower and change. As usual, the hot water heater in my barracks was not working. I suppose the idea of updating the men's barracks with post civil war era plumbing was out of the question. I took a painfully cold shower and dressed.

It had been a long day. I read every night before bed and listened to music on headphones. I had to wear headphones to listen to my music. Someone down the hall had no trouble sharing their rap music at ear splitting decibels for all to enjoy every night. I chose full ear pad headphones to block out the noise.

The room I shared with three other sailors was so cold at night that our breath drifted as mist in the dim light that shone through room's only window. I read for an hour or two and fell asleep on the thin, hard mattress. Two or three dark brown wool military blankets kept me from freezing to death until morning.

Great lakes was not an easy place to find love, adventure, or excitement. Sailors just tried to find some entertainment. My idea of weekend entertainment was a Saturday trip to the all you can eat buffet at Wendy's Hamburgers just outside the train tracks from base. For a kid with a few bucks in my pocket, this was a real treat.

After dinner I would wander further into town and end up at the local mall. There is no way to really describe the Great Lakes mall. Try to imagine that every fraud, grifter and shyster in America heard along the grape vine that a hundred thousand young naive sailors arrive in Great Lakes, Illinois every few months with paycheck in hand and not one brain cell in their head. The Great Lakes, mall was a spiders web of traps designed to take cash from new young men on their own, with money, for the first time.

Kiosks and shops lined the mall selling garbage that in some way appealed to young or patriotic men. Cheap and fake American Flag gem pins to send to dear old mom. Photo portraits in uniform to someday show your children. Replica firearms and outlandish knives.

My personal favorite was the home stereo system racket. These guys had you sign pre-written forms that deducted cash out of a sailors military pay for about three years to pay off this huge, at-home style stereo system with all the components. The cost was around a thousand bucks for this pile of rubbish from Taiwan. However, young mid-west guys who loved their music and never had a system like this before lined up to sign on the dotted line and take home a total stereo package. The catch 22 was that these morons lived in a barracks and ended up getting components stolen or had to ship the mess home anyhow.

Some kiosks were selling "complete professional camera systems" for sailors to record their world travels with. These cameras looked like 35mm pro style machines, but a closer look revealed made in China crap that was worth a ten spot at best. The shop would have tall and tight clothed girls pawning these cameras for about a hundred dollars. Oh yeah, they sold dozens a day. How could a young sailor who just spent eight weeks of boot camp with out seeing a girl walk by a kiosk full of smiling chicks and not say hello?

Getting by the camera kiosk was not easy. There were so many sailors in Great Lakes that the sales girls never remembered anyone. They may have hit on someone last week, but this week they were just another walking hard on with a pay check. After a month or so I realized how to get these kiosks girls to leave me alone as I walked by. First I would walk along the mall and let them draw me in. After talking to them about the product I would tell them how beautiful they were and ask them to marry me. I would act real serious about it. The sales girls would get so worked up and freaked out, they remembered me baby. I never got lured in by the counter girls again.

Weekends finished off with a bunch of diver wanna-bees getting together for pizza and beer at the mall pizza shop. I will never figure out how the shops were able to sell beer to minors. I guess the idea was that the sleazy bars were so close to base that the navy wanted to keep sailors in the cleaner and safer mall. Nice try.

While the last divers wandered back to base, I would stumble my way over to the mall movie house and choose between the midnight showings of Heavy Metal or Rocky Horror Picture Show. By the end of six months in Great Lakes I had both movies memorized.

Monday morning. I went through the freezing my butt off routine of marching to breakfast again. I filled my thermos with hot java and made my way to the training center.

Today I had a large manila envelope in my box. In fact, all of the engineers in my class did. Either the navy was sending our whole class to the western front or our post-training orders had come in. The orders contained the trainees first duty assignment. For the dive candidates it would give our designated dive school. I opened my envelope and sat down. Shouts and loud talk filled the rooms and halls of the training center as EM students who were preparing to graduate found out their next assignments.

Graduating EM's would be sent to aircraft carriers and destroyers in the fleet. Electrician Mates were in high demand at this time. Only a few of these young men would see shore duty anytime soon. Most of our class would be deep inside the hulls of steel war vessels roaming the seas of our planet. The graduating EM's would repair electrical damage and perform maintenance. Some would no doubt be injured or killed performing these duties. The work EM's trained for was dangerous and the voltage they worked around could light small towns. This was not a easy or safe job.

My friends and classmates talked about their orders and asked were I was off to. I pulled the white page from the manila envelope and held it out to read. Below the usual naval orders and notification jargon was the print stating my next duty station.

I was to report to the Naval Deep Sea Diving School on Ford Island, in Pearl Harbor, Hawaii. Silence. I could not even hear the sounds around me as students discussed their next assignments. I just starred at the word; Hawaii. Whoa.

Hawaii, to a mid-western boy, did not really exist. I mean, sure I may have heard an aunt or uncle talk about it from a vacation. Sure it was on the television or movies. Yeah, but it did not really exist, right? No one actually stayed in Hawaii, did they? Lived there? Stationed there?

I let it sink in and slowly I could hear the background noise of the other trainees talking. I was going to Hawaii for dive school. I spent my childhood in cheap military housing and trailer homes as my family roamed the United States. My father was a career man in the Marine Corps and later in the Navy. I never dreamed of going to Hawaii. It was just a late night television show or a coloring book. No more. According to the documents I was given, I would be there for some time as dive school could be several months.

Gordon, my friend and fellow deep sea contender, sat next to me and asked where I was going. I told him Pearl Harbor, Hawaii. Some place called Ford Island. He laughed and said he was going there as well. We had already spent six months here in Great Lakes together. It was nice to have a friend going on to dive school with me.

Gordon left on leave, vacation, before going to Hawaii. I was alone as I packed the remainder of my uniforms and rags for civilian clothes into my sea bag. The navy had so many uniforms. Blue ones, white ones, work uniforms, dress uniforms, heavy coats, wool hats, etc. There was barely any room to stuff my worn out Levi's and Budweiser t-shirts. Both were prized possessions of young navy personnel.

With my bags packed I went outside to catch a cab for the airport. As I walked out of the barracks building and made my way to the street, I could hear the ear splitting rap music wailing from the upper floors. The thumping beat sound filled the mud and rock courtyard of the decades old barracks. A pizza delivery boy, basically a sailor with entrepreneurial tendencies, basically a guy who needed extra cash to buy a car and get the hell out of this god forsaken mess on the weekends, ran past me with three pizzas and a goofy hat.

When I arrived at the street fronting my barracks a row of cabs were waiting for the sailors shipping out. I turned around, squinted and looked over the naval base. The sky over Great Lakes was gray and miserable as always. The brick buildings and muddy walkways had been my home for too long and I was leaving. I threw my bag into the trunk of a beat up limo converted into a taxi, and jumped in.

I was going straight to Hawaii, as I took leave after boot camp and before coming to Great Lakes. I intended to report to dive school and make a sharp presentation of myself. I had no idea what I was getting myself into or what was in store for me.

With a last look out of the taxi's back window, I said goodbye to Great Lakes, Illinois. The base guards watched me go as the white, sorry excuse for a limo drove by. I made eye contact with one of them briefly. We said everything in one glance. He knew I was leaving and I knew he was staying. Like a prisoner who just made parole, I rolled down the back window and shouted outside at the top of my voice.

"Free!"

Chapter 2.

This is dive school, dude.

Arriving in Hawaii was exciting. This mythical land across the sea was in my view from the window of my airplane seat. I watched the clouds clear and the islands come into view. The plane flew over Diamond Head crater and banked into Honolulu Airport. It skirted the light blue water of the Pacific and lined up over Pearl Harbor. The jet touched down and taxied to the terminal. I could not wait.

Just stepping off the plane a visitor is hit with the beauty of the islands. The airport is well designed to allow visitors to walk outdoors as much as possible. A courtyard full of trees and flowers brought sweet smells to the air as I walked by. This was amazing.

Many tourists were getting leis placed around their necks, fragrant strings of flowers, and being picked up by tour vans. The pretty girls in flowered dresses handing out leis were an amazing experience for me. I stared at the beauty of the Asian and Polynesian influences in them. They were so different from any women I had known until now. The Midwest and East coast life was not exotic by a long shot. Compared to this place I felt as if I had been choosing vanilla from the myriad of flavors available for too long.

While the tourists left the airport in limos and vans headed for Waikiki, no doubt, I made my way to the USO. The Honolulu USO office directed me to the waiting van en route to Pearl Harbor Naval base. What a drive. The green trees and palms. The air, warm and clean. Nothing like the dreary and exhaust filled air of the cities I had grown up in. It was a surreal experience.

Pearl Harbor was a real naval base and not to be confused with a training center or administration compound. Pearl harbor was the real deal. As the van drove into the base I saw huge destroyers and cruisers lined along the docks. Massive ships of steel with gun turrets, missile launchers and rotating radars. Welding slag poured from ships in dry dock flowing from sun-bright torches. Work crews scrambled around the base. It seemed as if the navy was in a constant state of upgrade and upkeep.

Grey vans and pickup trucks were driving to and fro with loads of men and supplies. Tall buildings made of modern construction were identifiable as barracks buildings for shore based sailors. It was a far cry from the life I lived in Great Lakes. Pearl Harbor was a place of action and purpose. Here ships were readied for war and defense.

The driver called back to me and asked where I needed to be dropped off. I told him I was new to the base and would be attending dive school here. The driver slowed down and gave me a look through the rear view window. Yeah, yeah…as usual, he was sizing me up.

There is nothing new about this. In the Navy, whenever a sailor tells someone they are a diver or going to dive school, they get checked out. The other sailors, non-quals as they were referred to, would look the diver over. Could they take him? Is he a tough guy? What was it about him that made him special? After a few years divers just get used to it.

Non-quals had a chip on their shoulder about divers and it took a while for me to find out why. Years after dive school I would realize what arrogant, big-heads many divers come across as. Hell, I did too. This was just too early in the game for me to realize this. To me, this driver was just eying me up.

Now this can often get explosive in a bar, you see. God help a diver if he is in a bar full of non-quals and chicks and it gets out that he is a diver. Some moron with a buzz-on is going to have to make a stand and show the diver up. In front of women it is a real one-up if a guy can tell off a diver in a bar.

For that reason divers never really show or talk about their qualifications unless they are in a group. Then divers have no trouble wearing loud and obnoxious t-shirts or hats. Its part survival, but more so it's a humility that a seasoned diver learns the hard way. By taking some lumps.

A good example of being sized up was in boot camp. I was not exactly Charles Atlas in Orlando, Florida during my boot camp training. I was a tall and lean guy who minded his own business.

During a physical training exam the diver wanna-bees were told to report to a special group in order to test for upcoming dive school fitness exams. One of the loud and trash talking members of my boot camp company could not help ridiculing me when I stepped out of the line up to take the fitness test. He called me every name in the book from skinny to puny and laughed the whole time. I felt like dirt.

As the testing began our group could hear the rest of our boot camp company beginning a fitness session. The company was lining up for a run. The diver wanna-bees had to do twice the average testing in boot camp and they were expected to go beyond the minimum requirements of graduation. The navy divers stationed at Orlando, Florida, boot camp, who gave the test to new recruits and dive hopefuls, told candidates that if they intended to just give the minimum expected of them in life they would never make it in dive school. Those boot camp divers were damn right.

Test after test beat the wanna-bees into pulp. Our group bled, sweat, yelled and clawed our way through each level of the exam. Push ups, pull ups, sit ups…anything that ended in "ups" were thrown at us to break our bodies and push our minds into giving up. At the end, the rabble that remained lined our sorry butts up for a final 5 mile run. The crazy thing was it would be in full Navy dungarees and steel toe boots. No tennis shoes or shorts allowed. With a shout from the test staff, the ragged group took off. This was it. Fail this run and no dive school. I had sweat most of the water out of my system and I was cramping hard even as I began. Damn! I was in good shape too!

After a few miles in the hot Florida sun, the first few runners started to drop. Those of us still able to move by the final mile turned into the home stretch that would take tus the rest of the way into the training barracks. I could see the finish line. The diver wanna-bees began yelling and cheering as our group knew we were going to make it. The size of our group by this time was about half of what it had been that morning. I would watch many good candidates drop out of training over the next year of my life. In Florida and in Hawaii. Diving is not for everyone. That's the way it is.

As I got closer to the finish line I saw a familiar face on the grass just outside of the course. It was Mr. Loudmouth from the company. Well, well. Tough guy himself had dropped out and was trying to catch his breath. Getting closer I realized that he was a team member none the less. It was not about the jeers and taunts. Boot camp is about being a team. Diving is about being there for your team. It is about not leaving a team member behind. I had to suck it up and do something.

The test staff shouted angrily as I ran off the course and rolled the young man up to his knees. I screamed in his ear for him to get up and run. Loudmouth was tearing and shouting with pain, the cramps had set in. Test staff grabbed my arm and told me to get going or else I would not finish the exam. I walked the limp runner for about ten feet and got him to start moving again. I shouted at him and even slapped his face a few times to get him to start running. Loudmouth began to move again.

When I finished the race I was amazed to see the previously downed runner finish behind me. My efforts had sparked something inside of the wisecracking jerk and he was able to get back up and run the rest of the course. He thanked me later and we became good friends during the rest of the training cycle in Florida.

The moral to the story is that divers may not all be muscle bound martial arts experts. Our strength is not measured by the size of our biceps. Under the worst of situations divers become their best. Divers fight and push until the test is over. They don't give up and they get the job done. What makes divers strong is deeper than skin and muscle. It is in the heart and mind.

Back to the gray bus cruising through Pearl Harbor Naval Base. The driver looked back at me in the rear view mirror and smiled to himself as if to say, "Oh, excuse me Mr. Diver sir." His smirk lasted a few moments just to make sure I saw it. So what. I thought to myself, "Just get me to my destination and I will never see you again, dude."

The driver took me beyond the tall, new barracks buildings and past the rows of warships. He drove well beyond the workshops and construction centers. Basically, the van left what I figured Pearl Harbor behind and kept driving. I wondered, "Where the heck are we going".

The driver drove past storage and warehouse areas. This part of Pearl Harbor seemed secluded and forgotten. The van turned up a road lined with old buildings. These structures resembled barracks from Great Lakes, Illinois which meant they had to be world war two era. Windows were missing and trees were cut down. This area of the base seemed to be designated for storage and may have been partially closed down. Why was he driving me here?

The driver asked if I knew what building I was in. What sort of question was that? No one lives here. This place is about two weeks from being leveled by a bull dozer. I told him I did not know and asked where we were.

"Dive school barracks." the driver stated flatly.

He must have to be kidding. Why would dive candidates be in the middle of desolation? This place was beyond even walking distance to any civilized, hell, populated part of the base. What would warrant placing dive school students so far from the rest of the world?

The driver parked in front of an old building and said this was my stop. He opened his side door, took my sea bag out and tossed it onto the cracked and broken sidewalk fronting the barracks. Without explaining, the driver jumped back into the van and took off. I was left standing there, alone, with my sea bag. I was standing on what was left of a sidewalk; next to a building that time forgot.

The wind, warm and clean, passed through the grouping of old barracks buildings. No real noise could be heard except for a door, somewhere, that creaked as the wind moved it. As I turned around and viewed my surroundings, I contemplated my situation. This place can not be right, I mean, where is everyone.

From behind me I heard a glass shard fall from its window and break into a million pieces. I turned to look in the direction of the noise. Just as I turned, a door slammed shut from the building next to me. I spun around again and looked. Nothing.

I picked up my bag and headed for the steps leading to one building's second level. This building in front of me seemed to be my stop, according to the driver. It was also where I heard the door slam. I walked slowly up the stairs and made my way down the cement balcony towards one of the rooms.

When I arrived at a closed door I noticed a picture torn from a Playboy magazine taped crooked to the window. Oddly, it was facing outside. Confused, I decided this was at least a sign of human contact so I knocked on the door.

No sooner had I finished the first knock, the door flew open. A dark tanned and seriously inebriated man opened it and stepped outside. Right into my face. He stood about two inches from me and reeked of about four different kinds of cheap whiskey.

"Ta' hell you looking fer'?" He burped into my face. This guy was about six inches shorter than me and wearing nothing but tan cotton shorts with brass ring ties in front. I would later find out that this was standard diver dress called UDT's.

Note: UDT is the old term for divers in the Navy. It means Underwater Demolition Team. The cotton shorts were brought into the Navy dive community at that time and worked very well. The shorts are still designated UDT's today.

My welcoming committee representative had several cuts and scrapes to his skin. He had not shaved for about two days and was bare foot. Pizza sauce wiped onto his cotton shorts proved that at least this man had eaten recently.

I began to stammer, "Uh...I am supposed to report to..."

"Dive school?" He finished my sentence. "You here for dive school? Well, well!" The man in shorts laughed and yelled back inside the barracks room. "Nubie, dudes!"

The room's door swung open and I looked inside. A television buzzed and crackled on the far end of the room with little to no sound. Its picture was black and white and lines made their way slowly up the image. The room's lights hung down from wires with just bulbs attached. Some lights were burned out while others flickered on and off like a bad connection.

Inside the room, three guys were drinking beer and other spirits. Empty and half full bottles of various liquors were laid all over the room covering the tables and floor. Pizza boxes and hamburger wrappers were strewn about. The three hombres inside were reclining on mix-matched chairs and sofas that appeared to have been thrown out by families who had used them for about twenty years, after another family had thrown them out.

All the men in the room were wearing the same tan UDT shorts and one guy had a blue ball cap on. They looked pretty messed up. In fact, they were about two days of drinking past being messed up. One of them raised his bottle of beer up to me and said hello.

In the background the leg of a fourth male stuck out from the barracks room's bathroom door. The leg's owner was face down, but still alive proven by an involuntary nerve twitch from the protruding leg every few seconds.

"Grey's the name," The man in shorts in front of me stated as he held out his hand to shake. "Welcome to freak'n dive school, dude."

I said hello to everyone and wandered further down the balcony, towards other rooms. Grey stumbled along with me.

"Just take a room, dude." Grey said, "Relax man, you look uptight. You need to chill. All uniformed and shit. Easy man, have a beer." Grey went on like this for about a half hour as I found an empty room. I unloaded my bag into the busted locker next to the bed.

Each room had a few guys in it. Some rooms were in various states of disarray. Others were kept neat. The neat rooms were kept up by a rather unique type of navy dive candidate. Neat freak divers tended to either be psychotic or Mormon. Regardless, they scared the hell out of the rest of the divers so we gave them plenty of room.

The dive school students, or candidates as they were called, inside the barracks were enjoying their weekend. Obviously, the work at dive school was tough so candidates were expected to get some sleep and have a few drinks on Saturday.

Grey wandered into my new room, "Hey, this room works. Nice. Here, have a beer. Loosen up. You cant have a moustache here, man. This is dive school. They don't allow it. Shave time, dude. Serious. Gotta go." Grey stammered and handed me a cold beer. I thanked him and took a long drink. With my bag unpacked, I changed into jeans and a t-shirt.

I leaned on the door jam to my room and surveyed the area. Now, with a keen eye and ear, I noticed people walking around the balconies of the various barracks buildings. Candidates were taking cases of beer and fast food up and down stairs. Overall, this place was not so bad. Hell, the toilet worked and the showers were hot. "Good enough for military work", as my dad used to say.

"Screw you!" Shouted a guy from two doors down. "I'll friggen'…" His words were cut short as a scuffle could be heard. Beer bottles could be heard breaking and a pile of, well, something, got knocked over. The whole floor of the building emptied out to see what was going on. Dive school candidates ran down to the room in question and burst in.

Inside two roommates were locked in battle. Drunk and lacking rest for at least a few days, the two rolled on the floor shouting obscenities. Various dive candidates pulled at them to break, but to no avail. Finally the whole level began to push and shove at each other as the fight became a riot. Laughter and yelling continued as the mob poured back out onto the cement balcony.

Music began to play as several boom boxes were turned up loud. The whole complex seemed to come to life as wanna-bees wrestled around the rooms. No one cared if windows were broken or doors tore from their hinges. The building was a mess anyhow. Now I understood why the Navy placed us here.

The dark of night closed on the complex and the party got more upbeat. Music and singing melded with shouting matches and the sound of breaking glass. God help anyone who needed to walk into the street or courtyard areas. They would be a walking target for beer bottles and half eaten slices of pizza.

I sat with a dozen guys whom I found out were going to class up with me for second class dive school on Ford Island. I gave a beer runner ten bucks and grabbed a few cold ones. Someone had opened five or six bags of chips and our group gorged on them hungrily. One of the guys handed me a few cold pieces of pizza from earlier that day. The t.v. in the room played some unknown sports game. All the classmates talked and got to know each other.

Candidates talked about their home states and training centers. Most were from engineering rates like me, but had trained in other cities. When I talked about Great Lakes, Illinois they laughed about the dismal life and poor weather. Our group all laughed together and poked fun at one another. This was a good bunch of guys.

When darkness came the building was well stocked for the night. Beer, hard liquor, pizza, chips, burgers, you name it. The dive candidates had nowhere to go. Several boom boxes were placed into the windows with good music playing loud. It was a combination of Southern rock and metal. These were the kind of guys who ended up here. Southern boys and metal heads. I fit in somewhere between the two. Dive school candidates were solid, American, young men and women who were ready to take on the world. First, they would have to survive Saturday night in the Pearl Harbor dive school barracks.

I ran back to my room and shaved off half of my moustache. I looked nuts, which added to my fitting in. The other guys laughed and the whole group began to tear the place apart. The Police arrived several times and did the usual drive through. It seemed the base police did not care what happened here. The patrol units just wanted to get back to the other side of the base. The clean buildings and quiet roads. This area was a mad house and the mad men inside were getting looped.

By two or three in the morning the music had been moved indoors and candidates sat in various rooms drinking and talking about dive school. Half of the group living here were in the class that was already in session. They were the senior students and the rest looked up to them. There were women amongst the candidates as well. Women could be deep sea divers, but not SEAL's. SEAL teams were designated as combat units and hard hat divers were not. The women had barracks elsewhere, but chose to party with the rest of their class here in nowhere-ville.

I walked around the barracks shaking people's hands and meeting everyone that night. I was pretty drunk by the end and finally made my way back to the room. Another guy who had taken an open bunk in my room that day was already sleeping half in and half out of his bed. I showered and passed out.

Sunday was a day of silence and recuperation. Sundays were an interesting day at dive school. The dive school candidates had their party weekend behind them which meant Monday was rolling around. Monday meant school. School meant sweat and pain, studies and tests, eliminations and drop outs. Mondays were reality. Sunday was the last day off before the class was definitely...on.

I sat on the couch in my room and chatted with my roommate. Gordon arrived and took a room as well. His leave after EM school was only a fast trip home to California and then on to Hawaii to make the start of our dive class. I spent some time updating him on the barracks. I introduced Gordon to several of the classmates that would be starting with he and I on Monday. The senior students explained to the candidates how to arrive at dive school the next day. The dress was dungarees and ball caps during school, but everyone started with physical training. That meant UDT's and running shoes.

At about lunch time the dive school students were awake and hung over. The barracks were too far away from the mess hall to walk, especially in the candidate's current state. To resolve this, the dive school, it turns out, had a flat bed, one ton truck that doubled as a troop carrier to get to meals. The dive school students piled in the back and rode off to the mess hall.

The candidates were all regular navy, but were attached to the dive school command which had privileges at Pearl Harbor submarine base. For that reason divers were able to use the sub-base mess hall and did not have to go all the way over to the main Pearl Harbor mess hall. This was a neat trick and a sneaky way to get a great meal.

The Pearl Harbor Sub-Base mess hall was rated as one of the top mess halls in the United States Navy. Sub base had real chefs who took their job seriously. The sub base mess hall employees called sailors sir or ma'am as they served up the best tasting navy chow I ever had.

The sub-base workers were all a class above the rest of the navy. Most sub base sailors were well educated and had high tech training. Submariners would go to lunch in sharp uniforms and neat head gear. Close shaves and clean haircuts were the norm for sub-base personnel.

It was a shake-up to say the least when the divers arrived in our flat bed truck. The candidates rolled up and piled out. Stumbling towards the mess hall and reeking of booze, no shaves, UDT's and steel toe boots, our group must have looked a mess. Once inside the divers kept quiet and took all the food we could. The candidates trays were filled with meats and deserts. Soda, milk, coffee...did I mention coffee? Candidates ate all they could stuff in them and made their way for the door.

Tired and full, the group of students piled into the truck bed and slept as someone drove the rabble back to the barracks. The rest of the day would be devoted to television and re-hydration. The senior students in the current class would go through flash cards and quiz each other for upcoming tests. Sunday was the transition time back to normal life.

By Sunday night I had my locker organized and my bed made. I took a final shower and crashed out early. I was nervous about my first day at dive school. At least I had a good crew classing up with me. Drifting off, I listened to the music playing from a room somewhere in the building and slept.

Monday morning I awoke to a loud knocking at the barracks room door. The time was 0630 hours and just getting light out. I rolled out of bed and stumbled to the door.

"Lets go people!" The shouts were from one of the senior dive class members. The senior candidates did not want anyone sleeping in and missing the ferry to Ford Island. The dive school staff wanted them to get the new class students to the dive training facility on time that first day.

When I looked outside I could see various dive candidates knocking on doors and talking with classmates. The whole building was buzzing with energy. I woke up my roommate and we got dressed for our first day.

The building emptied into the street below as students jumped into the back of our flat bed truck. Some of the senior class members actually had vehicles to take them to the ferry landing. Well, to call them vehicles is not exactly fair. These cars had been passed down for years to new dive school class members. No one really bought them, the cars just got handed down.

From one drinking buddy to another. The two and four door wrecks were in the worst state of repair. Paint was splattered haphazardly to create a bizarre look to the vehicles' exteriors. It looked like a mad artist had had their way with them.

The vehicles themselves had legends attached to them. Most of them were repainted after run-ins with the law in Waikiki. A chase through the naval base at two in the morning constituted a new paint job and possibly a new set of towels to cover the seats. On any given morning you could find dive school candidates passed out in the back of these cars. Heck, more likely passed out in the front with the motor running and the front bumper attached to a tree stump outside the barracks buildings.

Candidates climbed into these vehicles with colas and other high sugar and caffeine drinks in hand. By 0700 the whole group was winding its way through Pearl Harbor Naval Base towards the Ford Island ferry landing. The students parked the vehicles and off loaded. Other sailors waiting at the Ford Island ferry landing looked at our grouping of bizarre vehicles with expressions of confusion and disgust.

These ferry landings were for pedestrian traffic. I am not talking about the larger Ford Island ferries that are used to take vehicles back and forth. Those were located on the far side of Pearl Harbor. Near the Arizona Memorial and Submarine Museum. These ferries took personnel to work and school on Ford Island every day.

Every half hour a ferry came to pick up students and other Sailors. The ferry took a four or five stop trip around Pearl Harbor. It was the fastest way to get around by far. The candidates loaded themselves aboard the thirty foot boat and held on. The pedestrian ferries were not fast by a long shot and they bobbed side to side in such a way that you would tumble into someone if you did not get a hold of something. That's all a diver needed to do, half hung over and stinking, fall on top of a seated high ranking officer or something. Nice move.

In a few minutes our group jumped off at Ford Island and made our way for the mess hall. There was just enough time to grab a pastry and coffee before class. The senior students told the new class members not to eat too much because they will just lose it during PT, physical training. Heeding the good advice everyone downed a muffin and something to drink. A few brave souls had yogurt or eggs on toast to add to it. Some had to learn the hard way.

The Ford Island dive school entrance was just what a young candidate would expect. Two brass dive helmets and various lengths of heavy ship line were strewn about the entrance in decorative fashion. The line was braided and painted to give a traditional/nautical look that fit the school perfectly.

The building itself was definitely built during world war two. It was thick concrete in some areas and decades old corrugated steel elsewhere.

Inside the school doors, a visitor would find hundreds of old photographs and memorabilia. The school had great collections of dive gear used in years past. Mark 5 helmets, heavy dive suits and old face masks made of leather. Most of the senior divers who ran the school started with this stuff. Our class represented a new generation. Our equipment would be high tech in comparison to everything lining the halls of the school. I had great respect for those who came before me and dove this dangerous and experimental gear. Those tough hard hat workers broke new ground and laid the fabric for which divers now walk on. Many lost their lives with equipment that would fail or break under stressful conditions. Many still do.

In Administration, I filled out school entrance documents and medical history paperwork. I had taken the dive physicals months ago at the Great Lakes training center. A candidate could get washed out of dive school for medical reasons fast. One red flag and they are gone. It was akin to pilot training. Once a diver graduated they could get treated for problems or have their gear modified if need be. To enter school, however, a candidate must be a prize specimen.

Various dive school staff members walked in on our new class hopefuls as we filled out documents. The instructors did not taunt or laugh at us. It was not about degrading us or teasing. That would have been much easier for us to take. Instead the dive school instructors just walked in and looked. They leaned on the walls and just stared at us. Analyzing. Picking out who would make it through the training. The instructors watched the candidates quietly and did not smile, frown, nothing.

After a while each of the staff would walk out. In the halls I could hear them talking about the "new guys." Murmurs about certain candidates. Expectations were discussed just outside of hearing range from the class and it drove me crazy. The psychological side of dive school would be just as hard as the physical. I did not know that now, but I would soon find out.

After the paperwork, our class was told to find lockers in the locker room and change out of our dungaree uniforms. The instructors told the candidates to be on the grinder in five minutes wearing UDT's and running shoes. White t-shirts were given out with numbers and names spray painted on them. The numbers on the shirts were from one to one hundred. Each student put one on. The grinder was the huge cement slab behind dive school. Ford Island used to house world war two sea planes. This slab of cement sloped down into the ocean and made it possible for the planes to land in the water of Pearl Harbor, taxi to the cement slab and roll on up. It was a couple of acres of rough cement and in the heat of a Hawaii day, it became as hot as a griddle. It was nicknamed "the grinder" because many dive school students were ground down to failure on it over the years. If a diver slipped and fell on the grinder during PT, they wore a scar to show it. The grinder would be the physical and psychological wall each of us had to get over in order to graduate.

The candidates scrambled to get changed into their PT gear and onto the grinder. Clothing flew off in the locker room and everyone scrambled down the stairs. Staff members were there waiting, but they did not yell or scream for the class to get into formation. Instead they were lined up facing away from the school with their backs to our group. The instructors were facing out towards the grinder. The new class came to a halt, huffing and puffing behind them. The dive school instructors did not move from their positions.

One of the instructors, dressed in UDT's and running shoes like everyone else, raised his arm and pointed out towards the grinder. It was only about 10 am now but the grinder was a mirage of heat waves already. The air above the hot cement radiated as the morning sun had already baked it into a hot-plate. The instructors were all dressed for PT and they were in incredible shape. No weightlifters, no muscle bound Rambos here, just fine tuned athletes. Like tri-athletes with little to no body fat. Intimidating.

The class took the gesture by the staff to mean "get you're asses on the grinder, now!" So we did. Candidates ran out to the cement area, lined up in about ten lines and faced the instructors. None of the candidates had realized how many of us there were until now. Our group had a hundred men on this field at least. A huge class.

I stood at attention and faced the four staff members. The senior instructor, a dark skinned Polynesian looking man in top physical shape, spoke up.

" I am senior chief Kekahuna. You do not know me and I do not know you. Shut up and listen to what I am going to tell you now." He stated with a voice that did not yell but sounded out clearly all the way to the back row of our group. Kekahuna was in the kind of shape that could out-PT any one of our class. He had to be twenty years our senior and I suppose he could have taken our whole group out if he had a mind to. The senior chief's face was expressionless. His eyes were opened, just slightly, wider than normal. It was as if the words he spoke were getting him wound up and his eyes were showing it. Kekahuna did not frown or grit his teeth in any way. Other than the seriousness that shot from his eyes, he was in total control. Which basically meant he could blow up and be totally out of control in a second. Lesson one, do not screw with senior chief Kekahuna.

The senior chief spoke again, "There are one hundred of you that showed up for this class. There can only be fifty in the class that begins dive school." He stated this loudly and then just stood there.

I shifted my eyes and looked side to side to see if anyone had realized what that meant. Would there be two classes starting? Was our group going to be divided up and get new start dates? What the heck did this mean?

Senior Chief Kekahuna continued, " It is not your fault that this happened. The situation is that only half of you will stay and start dive school."

What? I thought. What is he talking about?

Kekahuna continued, "The other half will continue on to your next assignments in the Navy."

Our group of candidates was shocked. At attention no one could show it, but it could be felt. I asked myself, "How was this going to work? Hey, I did damn good in EM school. Top of my class. If the instructors wanted to review our folders I had a strong background. Lifeguard during high school, swim instructor in the Boy Scouts. I began to develop a file in my brain to present if questioned.

The senior chief spoke again, "We will find out this morning who stays and who goes. Again, this is not your fault. Too many of you were sent here for the class. Anytime you want to quit, just leave the grinder and go inside. Fifty of you will remain on this grinder and start the next dive class. End of story gentlemen. Let us begin." Those were the last words out of senior chief Kekahuna's mouth.

One of the instructors next to him shouted out to the group, "Assume the position!" This meant get our butts into push up position. Our group of candidates dropped fast onto the grinder and positioned ourselves to begin pushups.

I looked around at the other candidates. They were shocked and looking at each other with nervous glances. I thought , "Damn, what was this? PT until you give up? That was the selection process the instructors were going to use?" As I looked around I could tell the group of candidates were all in shape. Most of us had trained for dive school for years. I had been swimming and running daily ever since high school when I signed up for the Navy's early enlistment program.

The one hundred dive school candidates on this grinder had been training for this day for about…two or three years straight. Damn! This was going to get ugly. Real ugly.

"Be-gin," The instructor shouted out, "One, two, three, one. One, two, three, two. One, two, three, three. One, two, three, four…" Four count push ups. This would be the norm in dive school. Punishment of twenty push ups meant forty and so on. Every exercise was based on a four count system. Rough on the body and mind. I never really got used to four count push ups. They just suck.

The push ups went on and on as the candidates counted along with the instructor. "One, two, three , thirty. One, two, three, thirty one…." The strain in the student's arms and the heat on their bodies made mouths tighten and eyes bulge.

The push ups went into flutter kicks, a painful little dive school favorite where a diver would lie on their back and raise their legs one at a time in a straight leg flutter style. The performer never touched their heels to the cement. This exercise tore at ones middle. It just hurt. The abdominal strain and cramps this exercise puts on a diver is unnerving. "one, two, three, ten. One, two, three, eleven…" The flutter kicks went on and on.

The instructors shifted from flutter kicks, push ups, four count body builders (a mentally deranged form of jumping jacks that added a push up into the exercise. This can not be described well. Lets just say it hurt.). There was no stopping for water and there were no breaks. The morning went on and I just kept going. "One, two, three, forty three. One, two, three, forty four…" The candidates were getting knocked hard.

The noon sun was beating down on me as the heat rose up off the grinder like an oven. No where to hide, no shade, no break. It had been an hour and a half at least already and several candidates were shouting in pain as the exercises kept coming. I had resorted to screaming the count out with the instructors. It kept my mind off the pain and prevented the sensation of losing consciousness. It worked for the most part.

The instructors had not left the grinder the whole time. They were not doing the PT with the class, but they respected the effort and never took a break from the sun and heat. Instead they walked among the lines of men pumping out sweat and screams. They watched the group for injuries and failures. They corrected candidates on form and posture during exercises. No cheating here. If someone can not perform, they are done.

Each candidate had a pool of sweat under their bodies and the white t-shirts the instructors gave out with a number on it were dripping wet. Now understand this, the heat was high enough to instantly dry up any moisture that dropped onto the god forsaken grinder. Yet everyone had pools…pools of sweat under each of our bodies. The class screamed and yelled the cadence and shouted to each other to keep going. It was a last attempt to sound rational and team oriented. In the next hour that would all change and things would become personal. In the next hour, each of the candidates would fight for a position in dive school with their lives. Fifty candidates would lose.

27

Push ups, body builders, flutter kicks, sit ups, screams, pain. "one, two, three, seventy one. One, two, three, seventy two..." It went on and on. "push up position!" The instructors yelled. They took turns leading the PT session. Each instructor tried to out do the last. They were not even waiting to get to one hundred counts before changing the exercise. Instead the instructors changed at any time. After ten, after forty, after fifteen, it did not matter. They changed from push ups to sit ups after just two or three if the instructor wanted to. I yelled out in pain as I rolled over.

"Faster!" The instructors would shout, "Get into position or get off the grinder!"

Hour two. I was delusional with pain. Drenched in sweat. The pool of sweat beneath me was the length of my body. My legs and arms dripped sweat. It was instinct now, I had moved beyond the point of pain and rationality. I was a robot now. The sun was at high noon and soon the other robots would lose a gear. People were not going to hold up.

I never saw or even registered that people were lying on the ground around me. I just kept going. Push ups, sit ups, I did not stop to look at anyone. The count went on and so did I. I was in a zone far from this place. The grinder was a reality I felt on my hands, but I was not really there anymore. I was in automatic mode now. It was the ambulance siren that woke me up. I looked over from my position and saw two candidates being led to a big square military medic van. With hazy vision I could see the bright red cross painted on the side of the green van.

The sight made me look around the grinder. All over there were dive students down. Writhing in pain or getting sips of water from instructors with bottles. I saw them, but I didn't. I just kept going. I knew people were still going with me because I could make out their shapes in the sun. I had lost my clear vision already. Shapes and shadows ran past me. I just stayed on track. Push up position. Faster. Do it or get off the grinder. Sit ups now. Lets do it, quit, or go. Now!

By the end of the second hour there were about sixty candidates left. This was a dangerous place to be in. The last ten to drop would be tough. If the candidate made it this far they had no intention of going down. That is what it would take to drop out now. Literally going down. Each candidate left felt it. Any one of the remaining students could break now. It was sheer will and not strength that kept me going. Strength was a luxury long lost already. This contest was down to a mind game.

Push ups again, now sit ups. I wallowed in my pool of sweat. I bled from knees and palms where I had come down too hard. I had hit my head and chin on the grinder countless times. The cramps in my legs and lower back were like knives in my muscle tissue. My body was breaking itself down to find water and protein to keep going. I was eating myself from the inside.

Another candidate went down. Nine left. This candidate did not quit, he dropped. I knew that would be the case. He hit the cement hard and was removed. Another ambulance siren. I was grunting loud with each rep, each change out. I had lost my voice from yelling cadence earlier. Now I had to save my breath for my lungs, not my voice. The grunts I made would have to do. The noises were involuntary and meshed with the moans and outbursts from the other candidates.

The next few candidates to go out went voluntarily. This was the mind game now. This was down to who wanted it more. Several candidates walked off shouting obscenities at the instructors. Those students crawled off the grinder and laid down in the shade. Only a few were left to go. Anyone could drop now. I had to get through this.

"Don't stop!" The yell came from somewhere in our group. It was not loud and it told a story about its shouter's own pain. The yell was followed by others and soon the candidates were re-grouping ourselves. Class mates told each other not to give up. Push ups, sit ups, flutter kicks. The pain was so bad that I told myself to keep going out loud as well. I shouted out to the class and to myself , "Don't quit!"

The other dive school staff members and instructors came out from the school building and watched the remaining candidates. The senior class before us come out as well. They stood just off the grinder and watched our class go through hell. Candidates puked, they bled and sweat until their bodies shifted into heat exhaustion. The onlookers shook their heads and muttered to themselves. They pointed to candidates who were barely able to change into the next position anymore. Senior class members ran out to help those who failed to move and instead lay motionless in a pool of sweat.

It was nearing the end of the third hour. The fiftieth candidate dropped and was removed, by stretcher. The sky was clear over Pearl Harbor and the sun had no resistance before it. The heat baked the grinder. The sun itself looked down on the remaining fifty candidates without mercy. I had made it. The sun knew it, the instructors knew it, I knew it. I cursed the grinder and the sun together in my mind and tried to realize I had made it.

The candidates left on the grinder were told to come to attention and face the instructors. Sweat soaked, bleeding, clothing torn and shoes worn down flat from the cement. Our remaining group was a mess. I stood at what passed for attention. Candidates were delusional and many of them darted their eyes around to make sure it was really over. They were trying to see if anyone was still going, maybe they stopped too soon. I was nervous and I starred at the instructors waiting to hear the next position yelled out. It never came. It was over.

Senior Chief Kekahuna stood before us. At attention, he spoke, " You are dismissed gentlemen. Shower up. Eight am tomorrow morning, same place, in PT gear. Congratulations and good job." That was all he said and the instructors walked inside the building.

I looked around at the others in disbelief. The candidates were turning and looking at each other, panting and coughing. It had begun to sink in. I was breathing hard, gasping for oxygen. I looked at the far end of the grinder, through remainder of the group, and caught Gordon's face looking back at me. His shirt was shredded and he bled from his shoulders where he had been striking the grinder on position changes. He did not smile, neither of us could, we just nodded to each other.

United States Navy, Deep Sea Dive school, Ford Island, Class 9010 2C was formed.

Chapter 3.
The only easy day was yesterday.

For the first few weeks the new dive school candidates wore our white t-shirts with names and numbers on them. We had not yet started dive school until the present class graduated. The days were spent training to build our cardiovascular system and cleaning the school grounds.

Training included long runs around Ford Island. Not once, but twice or more times around the island. The miles were tough with the Hawaii sun relentlessly beating down on me. My class trained on the grinder every day after the senior class showered and went inside. During these weeks my class built the lungs and heart strength that would be needed to get through dive school's infamous first phase, SCUBA training and of course, pool week.

Pool week was always on my mind. The instructors never let up about how important it was to build our lung capacity and cardio system for this experience. No one in the senior class talked about their pool week. It was forbidden, basically to just cause a sense of tension.

The idea behind pool week was to weed out those who could not stay calm in a stressful and potentially deadly underwater situation.   Cool thinking and calm conviction would get our class through pool week. If a diver freaked out underwater during pool week, they were not going to the fleet. Pool week was considered a controlled environment where instructors could test a candidate's will and nerves. It was very real, let me tell you. There had been near deaths and injuries in pool week classes going back many decades of dive training in the United States Navy. The navy took diving seriously. Pool week was a right of passage.

This time period, before training officially started, offered the class freedom from the usual nightly study sessions and flash cards that senior class members were faced with. I could get off base to see the island of Oahu and cruise through Waikiki. Divers did not have the best reputation in Waikiki bars. Of course, divers did not have a good reputation anywhere else, now that I think of it.

On a Friday it was common to get out of dodge as fast as possible and load up on beer early. The weekend was upon the class and that only meant a few days to fit in all the trouble we had planned. Our class would finish our chores around dive school and take the first shuttle off Ford Island and back to the barracks. A smart few stopped at the sub-base mess hall for a final meal before hitting the town. Good idea. It would be warm beer and stale chips from here out.

Waikiki had many very well kept and well respected night life establishments where one could enjoy friends and conversation. Divers never went to any of them. I was more akin to the back row and alley way bars that were more my style. At that time, my style was to get sloshed and fight my way out of a place alive. This constituted a quality, well rounded weekend night.

My favorite bars were those off the tourist tracks. The places where the bartender knew my name, as long as it was Jerk. These bars were run down and poorly lit. Live bands, half baked on hash and booze, played all night. The walls were covered with license plates and surfboards from decades past. If I was lucky the restrooms had doors, those where the classy joints. Ahh, yes. Places like Anna Bananas, The Wave, Pink Cadillac and Gussie L'amour's to name a few. These were the warm and familiar surroundings of a dive class on Friday night.

Our class used the issued flat bed truck for all transportation purposes. It worked very well for Waikiki. The plan was to fill the back of the flat bed with coolers of ice and beer. Even when loaded with thirty guys or more this thing could haul out. Let me tell you, it takes nerves of steel just to ride in the back of a flat bed, drunk, doing seventy miles and hour down the freeway as the driver tries to compensate for the worn out steering system.

Once inside of Waikiki our group would park the truck on a small military reservation there called Fort Derussy. Fort Derussy did not have much to it, except a nice parking area. From there, the class was in the center of Waikiki which made Fort Derussy a strategic location to begin our evening.

Routinely divers would get thrown out of bars, hotel lobbies, dance clubs, liquor stores, tattoo parlors and cheap pizza restaurants. All the places that made Waikiki the family oriented place it was. For the most part, divers knew which places we could go to and which places probably still remembered us from the weekends before. Not that we could never go there again. Those establishments just needed a little more time to forget. Some places needed a little more time than others.

No matter what happened to me, no matter who I ran from or what trouble I got into, I knew the flat bed was there. It was the central meeting place for the class. Wherever the night took me, drinking, fighting, ralphing, escaping, whatever, I just had to make it back to the flat bed. By morning light it was loaded with passed out guys. Whomever had the sanity or sobriety to drive back took the task.

Meeting girls in Hawaii was pointless in dive school. For the average sailor stationed at Pearl Harbor I am sure it was fine. For dive school students, however, it never worked out. Guys would end up dating the same girls as others in the school and it would just cause fights. You see there are often women who are attracted to divers around any naval base. They know where divers hang out and who they are. One common disrespectful nickname for them was frog-hog.

Frog-hogs where the source of more fistfights, shouting matches, auto accidents and general entertainment than anything else in dive school. On any given weekend morning the usual suspects would be staying in one barracks room or another.

As frog-hogs intended to be, shall we say, of a unique personality (i.e. psychotic) they would often break into fits of rage or violent outbursts. These were followed by a volley of beer bottle projectiles and obscenities. Divers would run for cover and seek shelter in closets until they calmed down. Soon they would reconnect with their ever loved boyfriend/student of the week and all the world would be at peace in the barracks again.

With my love for films and what my class mates called "artsy-crap" I was able to thwart these outlandish relationships and meet girls at college hang outs . That way I did not have to deal with the unstable personalities. Instead I could meet nice, down home, American, suicidal, dark, depressed and alternative music loving chicks. Ah, sweet romance.

Even these never lasted. The stigma of being a young sailor in Hawaii was not a big plus for the dating scene. I was considered broke, cheap, car-less and un-cool. How false! I was not un-cool!

After I played the dating game in dive school for a few months I got over it. Dive school required me to focus. I needed to stay on track with my studies. Fights over girlfriends just hurt the team and dragged moral down. By the time the class formed up, we had our minds on graduating.

It was class up day and the start of our training. This was the day the candidates shed our white, jail house looking t-shirts and put on the official yellow dive school t-shirts. I don't think the navy had changed the yellow t-shirt design for about four decades. Our class could care less. Finally dive school was starting.

The training schedule was set and it helped to fall into a routine. Our class would pile into the flat bed each morning and set off to the Island, eat breakfast, and PT. Then we would hit the showers and attend classroom studies until lunch. The afternoon was more class room studies and hot coffee. Then, as usual, the class would swing by the base package store, load up on beer and chips and study flash cards until blackout.

The studies of dive school were not light. Diving physics included advanced mathematics and buoyancy studies. Laws of physical science and historical studies created volumes of notes and hundreds of flash cards. Fail one test and a candidate was out. As one dive instructor put it, we would be "kickin the can down the street pick'n our non qualled ass." Well put.

At the age of nineteen I did not expect to be studying Boyles Law or partial pressures of nitrogen. Huh? The way that gases interacted in a diver's body became very important. I was taught what symptoms to watch out for if I was experiencing nitrogen narcosis or cyanosis. I was instructed in the first aid and emergency procedures involved with dive related injuries and how to re-compress a diver stricken with the bends. Serious cases of nitrogen poisoning (bends) could cause nerve damage or even death. The lessons I learned were about more than just familiarizing myself with the diving world and science involved. The instructors were trying to keep me alive in what is truly one of the navy's most dangerous lines of work.

The main laws a young diver studies are:

Boyles' Law, which is related to the expansion and contraction of gases in the body as a diver descends into and ascends from the ocean's depths. Just as air gets thinner at high altitudes, it gets heavy under water and can cause problems when a diver tries to get to the surface to fast. The air expands quickly and can damage the diver's lungs.

Dalton's Law determines what concentration of Nitrogen and Oxygen is in the air a diver is breathing and how it changes at different depths. Too much nitrogen and a diver can feel intoxicated and even pass out underwater.

Henry's Law deals with how gasses, like nitrogen, are absorbed by the body. When a diver gets the "bends" it means nitrogen has been absorbed into their blood and is now forming a bubble as it returns to a gas form on the surface after a dive. A case of the bends meant the diver had to be thrown into a recompression chamber to pressurize the air around them again. It simulated being under water again, but in a controlled environment. The idea was to get that nitrogen bubble back into the blood stream so it can be removed normally through exhalation. I said this stuff was technical.

With each new course we took we made another stack of flash cards to study. Plastic flash card holders bulged with each class. Rubber-banded flashcards were carried everywhere students went. On the bus, in the barracks, in the mess hall. Candidates had no intention of failing a class. What a way to get dropped. If we were going to beat our heads in during pool week and work the skin off our hands every morning on the grinder, it would suck to get kicked out over a multiple choice question. Our classmates worked together and studied as a team.

To show our commitment to the school and dive program, our class agreed to shave our heads down to the bone. It was a real motivator for our group and received remarks of respect from our instructors. The only complaint I heard of came from the naval base police investigative division who had been tipped off that a group of sailors were starting a white supremest unit in one of the derelict barracks on base. After some explanation from our command and classmates the police left our group alone.

Morning PT had a new twist during dive school. The formed class members now wore our yellow shirts onto the grinder every morning for fitness training. The instructors thought that was just too pretty a picture to waste on the school yard alone. The class instructors took the candidates off the school grounds to PT. Our class became a walking, screaming and sweating recruitment poster for the navy's dive program.

Ford Island had hundreds if not thousands of men and women stationed on it. Various schools and other administrative commands were located in the buildings dotted all around Ford Island's lay out. Most sailors on Ford Island wore dress white uniforms and clean crisp hats every day as they roamed between buildings. The dive command was sort of the red-headed step child of the island. Whispers about dishelved and disrespectful dive students were abound. The other sailors on Ford Island hated that divers wore shorts and t-shirts as a uniform. The officers on the island hated it more than anything and often made complaints to the dive school command.

For that reason the instructors made it a point to take the current dive class through the Ford Island building complex during PT. Just imagine the site. Clean, white uniformed sailors jumping out of the road to let our class march or run by. Usually the instructors had already been working our class over for an hour and the group smelled horrible. Sweat, mud, saltwater and filth covered the students. Our bodies, faces and uniforms were a mess as we carried telephone poles through the well groomed complex.

If not poles we carried the instructors themselves, riding atop inflatable boats. My muscles strained to keep them at head level or higher as I called out dive school songs and a loud "Hoo-Yah!" The dive navy's unofficial call of the wild. Instructors constantly called out orders and cadence to give a good show to Ford Island's non dive school personnel. Of course, it was not bad at impressing the female sailors stationed on Ford Island either.

A common dive song our class called out was: (sung to a run paced cadence)

Blue.

> I had a dog and his name was Blue,
> Blue wanted to be a diver too.
> So I bought him a mask and four tiny fins,
> Took him to the ocean and I through his ass in.
> Well Blue came up to my surprise,
> With a shark in his mouth and gleam in his eye.
> Now Blue he be a diving fool,
> So I shipped his ass off to mixed gas school.
> Sing'n HooYah hey (Hooyah Hey)
> Easy day (easy day)
> Looks like another (looks like another)
> Easy day (easy day).

PT every morning could include running at full speed down and back up Ford Island's sloping grass hills and miles of cement roads. This was mixed with push ups, sit ups, somersaults down hill until a candidate regurgitated and other fun stuff. There was no end to the ideas PT instructors could come up with to break our group down and build us back up. I was constantly in pain and pushing myself further physically. The instructors were building my balance and my endurance.

A small pool on Ford Island was used to train our swimming and breath hold ability. Our swim muscles were toned to go faster and harder. Over-under exercises, basically holding ones breath from one side to the other underwater, built up our lung capacity. The instructors often tied my hands and made me either swim or perform bizarre tasks underwater. Retrieving rubber bricks and lead dive weights from the old mark 5 rigs were a favorite of theirs. Races between students and even between students and instructors were rewarded with promised food and beer that night.

A huge ships mooring line about a foot in diameter doubled for the telephone pole on days after it rained. The instructors left it outside to make sure it would be soaked and weighing a ton by morning. Carrying that damn lead-heavy rope around the island was enough to tear a student's shoulders from their sockets. The pain of carrying that damn twelve inch diameter line shot through my neck and back. If that hawser line couldn't take a team down, nothing would. After a month like this our class was in damn good shape and feeling invincible.

Good. Our group of candidates would need it. The first few weeks of dive school were tough as it included basic Self Contained Underwater Breathing Apparatus, or SCUBA training. SCUBA training ended, of course, with pool week. The instructors wanted our class walking into pool week feeling immortal with our new strength and education. The reality of our mortality would set in fast.

I did not talk much the mornings of pool week. There was not much to say. I knew I was walking into an unknown environment and situation. I had spent the last three or four weeks learning the basics of SCUBA operations. Emergency procedures, equipment checks above and underwater, night time navigation and search techniques were drilled into me. The steel navy scuba tanks and black rubber gear were familiar to me now.

Pool week would take a our class to the next level. Trained procedures would become instinctive reactions. If one of us failed to react, we would know it. Under water, confused and disoriented with no air is a very lonely place to be. The instructors told our class that there is only one rule during pool week, do what they say or quit.

What the dive school instructors did during pool week and how they tested a student's nerves had nothing to do with military procedure or regulation. There were no codes of conduct during a real diving emergency in the field. Pool week had to simulate a real emergency situation as much as possible to truly test the reaction of a student. That meant a pool week simulation had to be, basically, an emergency. The only way out was to successfully recover from the problem inflicted upon you and continue on or quit dive school right then and there.

Quitting was symbolized by placing an O.K. sign from one hand on a candidate's forehead. It seemed weird, but it meant that a diver could go no further and they were in need of air now. In pool week it meant a dive candidate was gone. In the field it meant a diver died. Maybe even took their dive buddy with them.

The class would start during dark morning hours loading steel tanks and gear onto the flat bed truck. No talking was needed as every candidate knew exactly what each had to do. By this time our class moved as a unit. The class leaders were guides and class members worked like a well oiled machine. We loaded the gear and got on the road.

For pool week the instructors took the training operation off Ford Island and over to Richardson Pool on the main Pearl Harbor Naval Base. Richardson Pool was closed for the most part as it was in ill repair. The pool sat empty and silent for most of the year. One or two old filter motors hummed quietly behind a cement wall. The pool itself was clean and still. For one week, however, about twice a year, Richardson Pool became a place were fifty or so young men and women would come to face to face with fear. Richardson Pool may have been closed and forgotten by the navy, but it would be remembered by me forever.

Arrival at Richardson Pool meant SCUBA station set up. Our class lined the pool with gear and tanks for inspection. The instructors knew how important this was to safety so they made sure everything was in working order. An equipment failure could get someone killed here.

Post-inspection meant buddy up and gear up. Buddies were paired different every day. I never knew who I would dive with. For that reason I knew how important it was to prevent fights and slacking during the first few weeks of training. Our class had to work together or we would not graduate.

My buddy and I got each other geared up. I performed a surface check on his equipment and he did the same for me. The same would be performed in the water and then again once on the bottom of the pool. My buddy held my pass or failure in his hands, as much as I held his.

The instructors had our group line up the first day in the water with our floatation vests filled. Candidates bobbed up and down waiting for the next move. Instructors huddled together and discussed the days events. Occasionally the pool week instructors would look over at the group and back into the huddle again. They would lock eyes with students and frown. Point fingers and make notes on paper. It was unnerving the way the mind games in pool week wore a diver down. Did the instructors hate me? Was this their chance to get rid of me? Did one of the school's divers take something I did or said in the past the wrong way?

The instructors gave a final set of emergency procedures in case someone had to be removed from the pool fast. Richardson pool had an ambulance parked outside every morning of pool week. I could not see the ambulance, but I knew it was there. Four or five instructors entered the pool after the students and gave our class the command to submerge.

Pool week was not a complicated theory. Two by two, the classmates held on to their buddies tight and swam around the pool. At each corner of the pool they gave a thumbs up signal to an instructor, thumbs up to their dive buddy, turned and continued in the circle. No problem.

The four instructors in the pool were there to observe the reactions of students when a "shark" hit. Sharks were the instructors that floated above the students on the surface of the pool looking down. A candidate was not permitted to look anywhere but straight ahead or at their buddy to check their gear. For that reason the team never saw a shark coming.

Shark hits were when instructors, or sharks, dove down and landed on top of a pair of students tossing them around, attempting to pull them apart and attempting to take one of their SCUBA tanks. A shark hit could include direct face hits, elbow or leg strikes, body slams to the bottom of the pool, anything. Remember, there was only one rule, do what the instructors told you. Period. A shark could and would knock the air out of a student and bloody their nose at any time.

Regulators would be torn from mouths and tank hoses tied up in knots. Masks were shoved down and hair was clenched in an instructor's hand to give them a handle to work with. Heads were banged together or on the bottom of the pool. I left the pool bruised and bleeding every day.

My buddy and I waited for the shark hits gripping each other tight and breathing nervously. I learned to never let out a full breath, afraid I would get hit just then. Instead I let out little bursts of air; taking it back fast and holding it. Skip breathing or "skipping" it was called. The instructors warned against it before our class started as skipping could cause a black out. Skipping was not a chosen technique; it was the bodie's reaction to fear.

Shark hits came to each dive team evenly to allow instructors to watch for uncontrolled reactions. Students who could get their gear untangled and working again without freaking out would pass the hit. Buddies had to hold on to each other during and after the shark hit. While a diver put their gear back on, they were expected to assist with their buddy's gear as well. This is where the over-unders in the Ford Island pool came in. The need for breath hold capacity was apparent. If a candidate could not get their tank and regulator clear in time, they would start to lose it and call for air. If an instructor had to give a student air, that student was gone. Pool week meant a diver either held their breath and fixed their gear or quit.

Hard work in the Ford Island pool, even after school, gave me strong lungs and long breath holds. I performed dozens of over unders on my own to build up my abilities. That kind of extra training paid off. In some cases shark hits could last almost a minute just by themselves.

I knew lung capacity would be a key to passing pool week. The first thing to go in a shark hit would be my regulator, of course. I needed a two minute or more breath hold to be ready.

I had it. I liked to do a little trick with the instructors by holding my breath and helping my buddy get his gear together first. When my dive buddy's gear was fixed and they were breathing I would then untangle my own gear and regulator. This technique would often take over two minutes from the time our team was first hit and lost air. The instructors would look down on me from the surface and from the corners of the pool and nod approval to each other. I could see the thumbs up they gave each other with my peripheral vision.

Each team of two could expect five shark hits every morning. The first two or three hits were tough and could shake a candidate into failure. The last few of the day were down right fierce. A student was tired already, breathing hard, scared, their hands hurt from holding their tanks and their buddy's straps. One's ability to stay calm and hold a breath on the last few hits was depleted greatly. These final hits were also the most violent of the day. No holds barred.

I left the pool with blood dripping from my nose that first day. I did not even notice. I was glad it was over. The instructors had our class line up for count. It was obvious that not all of the candidates were there. It was the first day of god damn pool week and the class had lost students! Some had quit or been dropped on that first day! The instructors told our class nothing about the missing students. Not one comment. Because the pool week instructors forbid any looking up at the surface of the pool, I never knew when anyone left or who quit. It was the end of the first morning and I was left. I was still there. That is what mattered and I had to stay focused on that.

Pool week was five days. From Monday to Friday the dive class loaded the flat bed, drove to Richardson Pool and set up dive station for the morning's operation. The process was repeated without variation. By 0700 hours I was in the pool, that day's buddy clinging tight to me, swimming circles around and staying sharp. Each day brought five hits and each day the class got a little smaller. To the best of my knowledge no one had yet left in the ambulance, but I would not have known anyhow.

On Friday the class was obviously smaller. Those remaining prepared our SCUBA tanks and geared each other up. I checked my buddy over for loose straps and fittings. All was in order and our team entered the water. Friday was the last day of pool week and I knew that the instructors were going to make it count. I fully expected to leave the pool that day badly bruised and bleeding. That was just fine. I told myself that morning that I was either going to be in the after class line up at the end of the day or in the ambulance outside.

The sharks made the most of the final day. I was shoved face first into the bottom of the pool, hard. My mask and regulator were tied together on the chrome covered valves of my steel tanks behind me. I bled from my nose and I think my ear, but each time I held onto my buddy tight and waited for the hit to end. Once the hit was over my buddy and I would begin the process of putting ourselves back together again and continuing on.

The fourth hit of the day ended with my buddy receiving a laceration to his shoulder when the shark spun his steel tanks so hard that the straps cut into my buddy's skin. The blood rose from the wound slowly and I knew he was shaken from the experience. His breaths were fast and I took some time to calm him down before our team moved on.

My buddy was still holding his shoulder as the two of us began to swim along the pool's bottom again. I looked over to check the wound and realized it was worse than originally thought. The muscles and bone under the skin looked as if the shoulder may had been popped out all together. The pain must have been excruciating. I knew I had to get our team through the final hit. Just one more.

I saw my buddy look up at the surface so I held his shoulder tight. I could see he was contemplating heading for the safety of the pool's surface. I reached over to him and grabbed a handful of his hair in my right hand. I pulled it firmly and brought his face directly to mine so that our SCUBA masks faced each other. I shook my head as if to say "no way, brother, not on my watch." My buddy nodded. He punched my arm hard as if to say thanks and we moved on.

I looked ahead of me and saw one of the pool week instructors waiving his hand in a hello gesture. It was a strange sight as the whole pool week experience had been so formal that seeing this almost humorous act was confusing. That was just what the gesture was supposed to be. As I looked at the instructor with a confused look in my eyes the final shark hit of the day struck my buddy and I. It was Senior Chief Kekahuna.

Senior Chief Kekahuna was a life long skin diving fisherman from the Hawaiian Islands. He was doing five minute breath holds when he was a teenager. His dark skin bore scars from decades of taking cuts and scrapes from coral and sea creatures. Those scars represented fights with eels and sharks to get his catch back to shore safely. Tossing around a couple of dive students was just plain fun for this guy.

My left hand was strained trying to hold my buddy to me as my right hand stayed firmly on my SCUBA tank straps. Kekahuna took turns striking my buddy and I and shoving us into the pool bottom. At one point, about a minute into the hit with no air, I looked over to see the Senior Chief actually straddling the back of my buddy like a horse and smiling as he rode him. My buddy's arm was swinging like a rag doll's, pain made him scream the last air out of his lungs.

At the end of the hit Senior Chief Kekahuna swung back over me and grabbed my neck. He struck the last air out of me and gave my side a final kick as he drifted back towards the surface. It was over. The hit must have been over two minutes. I looked around me and saw the redness of my own blood oozing from my nose again. Even without my mask on I could see the blood as a hazy shadow in front of my eyes. My side hurt like the ribs had been bruised or broken, but I was alive.

My first priority was to get air to my buddy who was scrambling to find a regulator. I swung off my steel SCUBA tanks and began to untie the complicated knot that Senior Chief Kekahuna had tied the regulator hose into. There was no time, my buddy grabbed my tanks and I knew he was just a few seconds from shooting to the surface. I needed to get him calmed down and focused on the situation. I grabbed his hair again and pulled hard. I actually brought his mouth over to the regulator of my SCUBA tanks and without untying the knot, turned the air on .

The valve was hard to turn with the hose tied around it, but I twisted it open enough to get air flow. I pushed the free flow button on the front of the regulator to get the water out and shoved it in my buddy's mouth. He breathed deep. I never let go of his hair for fear he may still make a break for the surface. After a few breaths he calmed down and the two of us worked on his tanks.

The process of fixing our gear took some time, but our team was moving again and getting a thumbs up from the safety diver who had been watching us from across the pool. His signal was telling us "Good job!" at first and then to go to the surface. On the surface I saw the rest of the class out of the pool and removing their gear. My team's final hit had also been the last of the week, no wonder the Senior Chief wanted to take it to the edge. Just my luck.

By the time we got back from breaking down dive station, cleaning and stowing the gear at dive school, the students who had been removed were long gone. They were even packed and out of the barracks. There was little to no chance of finding out what, when or how. It just was.

Friday evening, our class stood at attention on the grinder, behind dive school, on Ford Island. Our class was smaller, but those who remained knew and trusted each one of our team with their lives. Over the last week that trust had been put to the test . That was what it meant to work as a team and get each other through. More importantly, the instructors lined up in front of our class and told us they would dive confidently with any one of us. That meant more to me than anything else.

Senior Chief Kekahuna, who's breath hold ability as a shark played hell with us the last five days, called us to attention.

The Senior Chief spoke, "Gentlemen, outstanding effort. This concludes your SCUBA training and the first phase of dive school. Monday morning, 8 am, on the grinder in PT gear."

Class 9010 2C was dismissed from pool week.

Dive school moved into its second phase which consisted of actual hard hat style diving. The attitude of the instructors by this time was that our class members had completed the initiation phase of our training, each of us were now officially SCUBA qualified, so the instructors could talk to us and treat us with a higher level of respect. The students did the same, calling instructors by their names and even joking about our groups weekend exploits in Waikiki. The mood was more relaxed and focused on being safe more than being disciplined for various minor infractions.

Hard hat diving was the meat and potatoes of a deep sea diver's job. However, in the fleet, a diver could expect to work with a variety of dive gear. SCUBA was often used for basic inspections of ships and docks. SCUBA made up the first phase of most major dive operations. From there, divers would turn to heavier and more protective gear to dive deeper. Hard hat diving helmets and thick canvas suits offered the diver some cut and scrape protection form a rusted sunken vessel or a splintering dock beam. Hard hat suits did not protect a diver from being crushed under falling metal supports. Hard hat equipment also increased a diver's chances of getting tangled on the bottom or inside a sunken wreck. There were pro's and con's. Divers trained for the con's and hoped for the pro's.

The primary hard hat system that was used when diving was in its memorable hey day was the mark five rig. This was the old, tarnished, metal hard hat that is often seen in movies and cartoons. The mark 5 rig is the most identifiable hard hat yet made and has become the symbol of deep sea diving around the world. Round eye ports were cut into the mark 5 helmet to give a diver limited vision at best while working underwater. If a diver operated the mark five during their career they were most likely diving since Vietnam. The mark 5 dive system had taken the United Stated Navy through most of the wars during the 20th century. Several militaries around the world still use a form of this rig.

The United States upgraded to the Mark 12 gear around the Vietnam era. The Mark 12 was the son of the Mark five as it was based around the idea of a big pot on the head with eye ports. The Mark 12 was fiberglass and metal making it somewhat lighter, but still strong and protective. The eye ports were squarish instead of round and it had a big, easy to look through front window plate. The Mark 12 was the main rig our dive school students learned on in deep sea training at Ford Island as the newer Superlight 17 hats were just arriving into the fleet.

Before I talk about the Superlights, let me explain more about the 12's. When a diver was fully geared up in the Mark 12 hat and attached to the heavy, water tight suit, they felt high and mighty. Divers were more confident to go after deeper and more dangerous jobs because they felt as if they were in a protective capsule. The mark 12 suit had lead weights to keep a diver negatively buoyant and give them the ability to walk on the ocean's bottom.

Metal knobs on the right side of the Mark 12 helmet kept the air flow into the helmet and suit adjusted. Increased underwater labor meant a diver needed more air and more oxygen. Divers also had to flush the old CO_2 contaminated air out of the helmet now and then to keep themselves from blacking out. This was a procedure called "ventilating."

Modern hard hat dive gear like the Mark 12's and Superlight 17's have the ability to communicate with the diving supervisors and dive station team above water. The supervisor and master diver on the surface, on dive station, could discuss operational procedures or exchange ideas with divers working on the bottom. In order to keep the salt water from screwing up a diver's communications, or comms, dive station workers filled every connection from the surface to the microphone in the helmet with a white, silicone based, water displacing goop. Dive rig comms were a touch and go system at best and often divers just relied on the old standard of pull signals to get a message through to the surface.

Pull signals were the original comms of the dive navy. A diver would give a series of tugs on the "umbilical cord" (air and comms lines tied together) to relay a message on to the supervisor and vice versa. If a diver was in SCUBA they could use an attached line to do the same. As the comms on deep sea rigs could go out at any time, and often did, divers had to stay up on their pull signal knowledge. If the dive station supervisor on the surface signaled for a diver to turn left and instead they turned right they could find themselves walking into a moving piece of machinery or some other danger.

Deep sea divers learned to set up dive station from start to finish and repair everything involved with it. Air lines, comms lines, filter and pump systems, suits, everything. A master diver wanted their divers cross trained in repair and operation of dive equipment. If one diver went down with the bends during a dive their position could be filled by others.

Instructors drilled our class in dive station set up and breakdown procedures. The instructors watched our repair techniques to insure quality work. Dive school emphasized attention to detail. A diver's life depended upon work being done right.

After working both above and below water with each dive system our class moved to open ocean. Ford Island was able to only offer shallow training dives off the cement perimeter wall. To get deeper the instructors and our class would move the gear onto a converted navy workboat that was set up for dive operations. The old, gray and flat topped work boat was about fifty to sixty feet in length and contained a recompression chamber inside. Having a hyper baric chamber on the work boat made it possible to both train and treat divers at sea for the bends.

All divers had to be qualified in working a recompression chamber. Each member of the class took turns loading a simulated injury inside the chamber, supervising the pressurization of the chamber to simulate depth and giving aid to the stricken diver. Recompression therapy could take hours in real medical emergencies. The idea behind the recompression of the air around the diver was to simulate the pressure of being under water again, thus returning nitrogen bubbles in the bloodstream back to a state where they could be released by the body normally through respiration.

When a diver came up from a long or deep dive, it was possible that nitrogen was trapped in their blood stream. Nerve system problems or damage that nitrogen bubbles could cause were known as the bends. Facial ticks, muscle spasms or loss of sensation in a limb were common signs and symptoms of the bends. The more serious bends cases could cause blackouts or even death.

From the workboat our class was able to make deeper dives into the blue, clear water of the Pacific ocean just outside the mouth of Pearl Harbor. The diving around Pearl Harbor, Hawaii, was beautiful and offered almost unlimited view into the distance while on the bottom. A diver looking up at the tiny workboat bobbing above and the umbilical cord winding its way from them to the surface was an awe inspiring site. A dive school student really felt like a deep sea diver here. The same way that a navy fighter pilot always itches to fly, divers always want to be one in the water. The ocean was home for a diver and we felt comfortable there.

Dive school had to get a new diver ready for the real work they would perform in the fleet. Second class divers could expect to weld, grind, bend rods, tie chains and even cut metal underwater on any given day. This was more realistic to their fleet duties. Welding and underwater repairs on ships were a diver's primary mission. If any members of our class were assigned to photographic or demolition teams they were lucky. The bulk of our class would earn their paychecks banging steel plates into place under ships and welding the plates on with oxygen acetylene torches.

Hull inspection and repair was better known in the navy as "ship's husbandry." Ship's husbandry did not have a glamorous sound to it. A work week of ship's husbandry could wear down a diver's mind and strain their muscles.

The other sailors in the navy never really saw what divers did underwater. Dive boats would show up in the morning before light and by that evening all anyone on board the ship would have seen was a bunch of multi colored lines dangling into the water. For this reason a diver's job was often viewed with confusion by the rest of the fleet sailors. However, if a billion dollar guided missile cruiser could not get underway because of a problem below the waterline, divers suddenly became the knights of the round table. A ship's captain would prepare meats, desserts and hot coffee for our divers in order to get the job done fast.

Ford Island dive school was well equipped to get us trained for ship's husbandry. A huge water tank gave our class an above ground training facility to learn in. Instructors had dozens of mind bending and bizarre dexterity tests to give our class underwater. Timed tests were given such as assembling metal flanges and bolts on steel plates with our dive helmet's viewports blackened out to prevent vision. Our class had to simulate working in the worse conditions possible.

Wrenches were tied to our belts to prevent loss if a diver dropped them. Screwdrivers were tough to manipulate with heavy air tight suit gloves on. One test after another was given to push our skill levels higher in underwater tool handling and repair. Our class used drills, sledge hammers, torches and a variety of custom tools invented by divers before us to perform ship's husbandry simulations.

Each test was more complicated and required greater concentration and dexterity to complete. Failure to pass these tests could mean failure of dive school altogether. After all, if a student could not do the job, they could not be sent on to the fleet and dive commands. Most naval repair facilities were located in cold, dark, coastal water areas. A diver had to be able to get a job done by touch , not sight and on time while freezing their ass off.

Divers were designated by colors to keep them straight underwater. Divers were assigned as blue diver or red diver with another diver, green, waiting on the side as a stand by if there was a problem on the bottom. Tangled umbilical cords or a diver in distress would require the standby diver to be deployed. In dive school the standby diver was another student in full gear ready to go at a moments notice as navy regulations required. In the fleet, at dive commands, the "standby" was often the one guy who showed up that morning on dive station still too drunk to dive so the supervisor propped him up against a wood post on the dive station with a set of SCUBA tanks strapped to his back.

Diver's had color coded umbilical cords to match their color designations. Everything was designed to keep dive stations neat and orderly. By god this stuff was starting to make sense.

On the dive school work boat a comm-set would crackel an unintelligible message every few minutes to which every one on dive station would turn to see if the dive supervisor had understood. The supervisor did not, most likely, but would not dare say so. With a nod from the "supe" our class would all continue with our positions on dive station.

Each student took turns supervising the various simulated underwater missions. Divers would inspect dive gear and run the stop watches during the dives. Supervisors wore stopwatches to keep track of the amount of time a diver was underwater and to help with tracking a recompression chamber therapy. Supervisors had to keep track of depths and bottom times to prevent the bends as much as possible. Dive tables and navy regulations had to be memorized and recited often to ensure the instructors that our class knew what we were doing.

The second and final phase of deep sea school came to an end with our deep dive certifications. Our class had already shown our proficiency in metal work and repair. Our supervisor and hyper baric chamber training was complete. The members of our class were confident. On our final day the work boat was loaded for a the day and headed for open ocean.

The deep dive certifications required our class members to set up dive station ourselves. Each student geared up each other and took turns supervising our own dives. Instructors watched from the rails of the work boat and took notes for the critique later.

47

Our objective that day was to achieve a depth of 190 feet on air. Our class independently set up, operated the dive station, dove and broke down the equipment while the instructors observed closely and commented on our actions quietly to themselves. The dive school instructors were always there to keep an eye on our class, but by now we were experienced enough perform dive station with little to no guidance. Our class was effective, capable and ready to graduate.

After my qualification dive I would never forget the experience of being fully suited up in the Mark 12 rig and looking up at the surface from 190 feet of pure, clean, Pacific ocean water. I watched as schools of silver fish drifted by. Many were huge, mahi or Hawaiian ahi (tuna). No doubt the fish were curious about me as well. Here was a stranger in a bright yellow suit and a long cord to the surface wandering around their domain. Now it was my domain as well. I would officially become a "denizen of the deep" as my dive school graduation certificate would read.

The clear water of Hawaii was perfect for diving. Being able to have completed dive school there was a blessing for me. For many of my fellow students they would never have these kind of comfortable temperatures and clear water conditions to dive in again. My graduating class would separate and many would travel to bases with cold and muddy water on the northern Atlantic and Pacific coastlines of the United States.

My dive buddy during my qualification dive pointed out what appeared to be a large and slow moving shape in the furthest distance of our underwater vision. The shape was a lumbering shark that may have just finished a big meal. I would have been frightened on any other day, but with dive school ending I was full of adrenaline and just enjoyed watching the big fish swim, semi-circle around us and wander off.

I should mention a little known agreement that navy divers have with sharks. For generations navy divers have agreed not to eat shark meat if, in return, sharks agreed not to eat us. This tradition sounded corny to me at the time, but I did not and still do not knowingly eat shark in any form. The agreement has worked so far so why mess with it?

With our 190 foot dives on air in the Mark 12 suits behind us and officially in our service jackets, our class was dismissed for the week. Monday would bring our new duty station orders. Graduation would be a few days later.

By now, a new class of candidates were wandering around the dive school grounds cleaning and maintaining the equipment. The junior students wore the white t-shirts of a non classed wanna-be. Numbers and names were spray painted on these white t-shirts just like the ones our class wore when we first arrived at dive school.

There had been no mistake in orders this time and the correct number of students were sent for the next class to be formed. The junior students would not have to go through the elimination day on the grinder that my class had to. The senior students did not rub it in or place ourselves on a pedestal because of it. I would not have wished that experience upon anyone.

The final weekend of dive school was upon me. Save being picked up by the police for running naked and drunk through a Waikiki hotel lobby, I was not going to be kicked out of dive school for just about anything now. I was home free and work free for the next two days.

Once dismissed from the qualification dive week our class turned over the dive school's cleaning chores to the new candidates in white t-shirts and headed out. On the way to the barracks our class loaded up a shopping cart with beer and various unhealthy salt covered and deep fried potato products. The shopping cart had been commandeered weeks ago by one of our class members and we kept it hidden in group of trees behind Hickam air base liquor store.

The word had come down that the barracks our class was in would be leveled to make way for newer facilities. The new dive class had already been moved to other locations and I was told to load up my belongings for the transfer. As our class drank beer we loaded the old, beat up flatbed with our sea bags and any excess furniture. Classmates wrestled and body slammed each other into the walls and doors with no care of what damage would result. The senior class blasted music and basically trashed what was left of the building.

Looking like a scene out of the Beverly hill-billies , our class piled on top of the mound of furniture and clothing and the flat bed truck took off. Dressed in dive school shirts and tan UDT shorts, our class waved to Pearl Harbor personnel as we drove through base with beer cans in hand. The heavy and unstable truck took out corners and curbs as our class held on for dear life. I was pretty sure the new barracks would have rooms waiting for our group on the far side of the base. That was what we were told anyway.

The flat bed had lamps and chairs tied to its sides. Sea bags were piled on the hood and filled the passenger side of the cab. With limited visibility at best the driver careened through the base barely making turns and stop lights. Beers were handed from one student to another and potato chips were emptied all over the pile of goods as we chomped on them for dinner.

Sailors and officers walking by the flat bed's path looked at our group and shook their heads. Officers pointed and frowned at our actions. Yeah, yeah. Look, we were freakin homeless, leave us alone. At one stop light, and officer tried to get our command's name, but the driver tore off at the green light losing several beer bottles and a chair from the flat bed's load. A glass bottle smashed in front of the questioning officer as he shook his fist at us and yelled obscenities.

In an hour our class located the right barracks building for our new quarters. It was decided to send in a scouting party to assess the situation, leaving most of the class behind to protect the possessions and beer from theft. After an hour of listening to our boom box play and getting odd looks from sailors returning to the well kept barracks building the flat bed was illegally parked in front of, the scouting party returned, at a run.

Apparently one of them had hit on another sailor's girlfriend and started a fight, in one hour! The barracks security person was chasing the scouting team as well as a dozen other screaming sailors. Without delay our class held on to ropes and gear as the big truck fled the scene.

Unsure where to escape to our group doubled back through the base and over to the Ford Island vehicle ferry. Ford Island would be a good escape for us. The senior class remained in the Ford Island barracks until the end of school. The Ford Island barracks were old and in very poor condition, but they were far from the eyes of the regular navy types. The Ford Island mess hall was just next door so the old barracks had their advantages.

On Monday our class had sobered up and were ready to get our new orders. The senior class candidates had spent the weekend talking about different naval bases and ships that had dive detachments. Far away and exotic commands in Europe and Asia. High tech commands and special units. Anything was possible.

What would be our first duty assignment as United States Navy deep sea divers? Let me explain exactly what dive commands are.

There were many commands that a young diver could be sent to in the Navy. Divers at these various commands were used in different capacities. Some were directly tied to repair facilities while others assisted research and development commands. Dive commands were often referred to as "dive lockers".

The first level of dive commands were the most glamorous. At the top was the National Aeronautical and Space Administration command in Huntsville,

Al. Navy divers stationed at the Marshall NASA training base helped to train future astronauts in huge water tanks that simulated zero gravity conditions. This command was often featured on news and documentary shows and was a prized command to receive orders to.

The first level also contained the elite special projects command and Panama City Florida dive commands. This was the real show in the United States naval diving world; cutting edge dive systems and experimental gear. The Panama City command trained the mixed gas divers and dive officers right on the ocean and was just steps from Panama City beach, one of America's premier party destinations. Orders to Florida were orders to dream for.

The second tier of dive commands were called dunk tanks. These were aptly named for their function of training navy and air-force pilots in water ditch escapes. Divers would work as trainers and rescue swimmers if the pilots involved could not get free from the cockpit simulator. The pilot goes into the water, gets free from their harness and swims to the surface. Dunk tanks were located on or near major air bases and offered a nine to five schedule with little heavy work involved. Not to mention plenty of cute pilot chicks to hit on.

From here on down divers actually had to start working. By working I mean keeping the damn fleet running. Remember, we are "navy" divers…like as in part of a fleet of ships and all. Those who were stationed at the following commands sure as hell new they were navy divers as they worked on ships for a living. It also meant they did not know anyone in the right places to get stationed where they did.

Level three commands were shore based submarine and surface vessel repair stations. These often gave the divers a chance to start a relationship off base and even live in a real apartment. Luxuries like these would end at this level. They dove every day inspecting, repairing and replacing parts on ships and submarines. Their commands were often well kept and well equipped.

The dive locker at submarine repair base Bangor, Washington will always be one of the most beautiful commands and bases that I had experienced in my navy career. The cool Washington state air, thick green trees and distant mountains gave the Bangor dive locker and old world mystique feel.

This takes us down to the level four dive command. These were the submarine and destroyer repair vessels. Huge ships stocked with heavy welding and fabricating equipment. It was often said that each of these vessels carried enough supplies to actually build a destroyer if they wanted to. Inside these ships were complete diving commands with chambers and loads of diving gear. They could become a repair facility anywhere in the world if they had to so they were well stocked and staffed with dive personnel.

They were also non-combat ships, which meant they were well stocked with another valuable piece of naval equipment, female sailors. Submarine or destroyer tenders were often over fifty percent female staffed commands. From the captains on down they were used to give women the sea time they needed to move up in rank.

With most divers being male, about 90 percent or more, being assigned to a tender can be a ticket to have plenty of fun. That is, until they get arrested, accused or otherwise see their career go down the toilet. Remember the old tale about being careful what you wish for?

Below tenders, well below the shore commands and out of even visual range from the level one diving commands, came the salvage boats. Junk boats as they were referred to in the navy. Junk boats were designated as ARS or auxiliary rescue salvage vessels. These ships were the last place a diver wanted to get assigned in the whole freaking show.

Most ARS class ships were built in world war two and had already been decommissioned a few times only to be re-commissioned when the navy realized it was cheaper to operate their own salvage ships than outsource to civilian corporations. Some new ARS vessels had been designed and even a few built at the time of my dive school graduation. For the most part, though, if a diver was sent to a junk boat, they were bunking in the same bunk their grandfather, who fought in WWII, bunked in. If the navy is given a billion dollars to upgrade its surface vessels, do you think it is going to the nuclear carriers or the ARS fleet? You get the picture.

Lets put it this way, two years on a junk boat meant four years of sea duty to the United States Navy. The work was tough and the living conditions were horrendous. State prisoners were allotted more bunk space than a sailor on a salvage ship. Heck, even the officers shared staterooms on these tubs. Let me tell you, after spending time being treated like a prince at another command, officers were not happy to walk on board a salvage ship and grab a top bunk. As usual, it all rolls down hill. The bad feelings started at the top and worked its way down to the bottom.

Our class sat down Monday morning, coffee in hand, a luxury given to those students who were entering the last few days of their training. Instructors filed in as well and leaned on the walls. The instructors had spent years in the diving navy before being assigned at the school so they were just as interested to hear the results of our class's assignments. The envelopes were brought in and passed around.

Our dive class was dressed in a combination of blue dungarees and green "sea bee" construction uniforms. The green uniforms were not worn by any diving commands any more except those connected to navy construction or "sea bee" units. Training commands could wear them as well if they wanted to, but in Hawaii the more comfortable UDT's were preferred. This was the only time that many of us could wear the cool all green uniforms of the old dive community. Myself and others had sets made to wear this last week. We wore them all over that base with pride.

Several students tore into their envelopes fast. They read aloud commands like Panama City, Florida and San Diego, California. Others were going to submarine repair facilities in Connecticut and right here in Pearl Harbor, Hawaii. The commands were read one by one. Students were going to Norfolk, Virginia, the worlds largest naval base, to work at ship repair centers.

Finally I opened my yellow manila envelope and pulled out the computer printed orders sheet inside. Some instructors gathered around to read with me. The assignment inside read as follows: Upon completion of Second Class Dive School, blah blah, will proceed upon graduation or after leave time is taken, blah blah, there it was….USS Reclaimer, ARS 42.

Everyone was silent for a moment. Too long a moment. The instructors shot looks at each other and then gave light pats on my back. They gave bland and unbelieving congratulations to me on my new assignment. Some said it would be a character building experience as others just nodded with half smiles and walked away. Across the room I saw Gordon looking at his assignment sheet.

Gordon and I had been in electronic engineering school together and now dive school. I figured I would walk over to him and see where he was going. As I sat down next to Gordon he looked up at me and spoke, "Reclaimer? That's a salvage boat, right?" He was trying to convince himself that he was not dreaming and that he was indeed just given a two year tour on a navy junk boat as his first command out of dive school.

"Yeah, it is." I told him. "See you there, bro."

Gordon looked at me surprised and read my command assignment papers, USS Reclaimer. We were both reporting to ARS 42 in about one week. Gordon began to laugh and I had to join in. Again I have to say, I never would have been able to make it through such a crazy assignment as the Reclaimer if Gordon had not been sent there as well. We would have to go through this together.

One positive side of the Reclaimer assignment was that it kept us in Hawaii. The Reclaimer was stationed in Hawaii on the far side of the harbor, alpha docks. This was a little known naval installation at the tip of Hickam Air Force Base next to Pearl Harbor. Gordon and I liked Hawaii and we took this as an upbeat spin on our orders.

The excitement of the commands took up the morning at school and we were dismissed to plan our leave time and travel needs. The class poured out for lunch and later met up in the Ford Island barracks where we were hiding out from the rest of Pearl Harbor. Talk about the new commands were abound. A few instructors had come over to join in some beers and discuss their experiences from years past. The submarine bases and training commands were ideal assignments and would provide ample time to go to school at night. The instructors never offered any advice to Gordon and I. We would have to figure this out on our own.

A week later Gordon left for leave to see family in California. I packed my sea bag and, without any family leave time planned, hitched a base transport ride to the far side of Pearl Harbor. Good bye dive school and Ford Island. Good bye to the instructors and the damn grinder. From here on out I was a junk boat diver.

I felt a sense of both concern and pride as the big gray bus drove along. The Pearl Harbor ships were lined up, clean and ready for action, outside the bus windows. Destroyers, missile cruisers, and submarines were all freshly painted with bright white numbers marking the bows. Sailors in dress white uniforms manned the quarterdecks of each ship to greet those who arrived to visit or repair ship equipment. These ships were the backbone of world stability and national security. They looked it. They were clean and mighty looking.

The bus reached the end of Pearl Harbor and the driver called out to the passengers that we were entering Hickam Air Force Base. Hickam and Pearl Harbor are separated by a common steel boundary fence. The USS Reclaimer was moored at the end of a long road to the ocean cutting through the air base. Let me tell you, once I cross that fence line, I knew I had entered an Air Force Base.

Hickam was not the cement and steel environment of Pearl Harbor. Naval bases are maintenance and repair stops for ships. Shipyards do not intend to or try to be glamorous, well appointed and landscaped. They have a factory and scrape yard look to them that makes sense to sailors who performed heavy repair work on vessels there. Hickam, like all air force bases, was very different.

Hickam AFB was green grass and groomed trees. The gray transport bus I rode on even looked out of place here. The well groomed yards of command buildings and officer's homes gave Hickam an almost movie-like appearance. Many of the concrete buildings on Hickam that were built prior to December

7, 1941, were still in use. The Air Force had repainted them but they did not repair the damage to the concrete walls from Japanese fighters as they shot up the air fields. The damages were left as a reminder of the attack.

Everyone got off the bus as we stopped along Hickam's long roads. Just I remained. The driver knew where he was going, thank god, because I did not. This was all new to me. In the distance I could make out the mast of a ship. Clustered around the mast were huge metal warehouses and fence lines. It had the distinct look of a naval yard and was easy to spot from the green and lush air base around it. The bus drove right up to the naval yard's security hut and stopped.

I thanked the driver and drug my sea bag off the bus. The bag made a puff of dust and dirt that whirled around me from the unpaved parking lot fronting the naval yard. With a grind of gears the gray bus backed out of the area and drove off. Dust blew all around me from the tires and I covered my eyes to keep as much out as possible. I coughed and waved my arm in front of me as the bus took off.

When the dirt settled I turned towards the base. A metal sign that needed repainting, years ago, read "Alpha Docks" . This was it. I could see the USS Reclaimer past the security gate. The ship was identifiable by its white 42 on the bow. The ship was not too long. Probably just long enough to be designated an actual ship and not a work boat. Two masts shot up from the main superstructure with a spider web of steel cables running down from the top of each. Some of the cables appeared to be for support when underway and taking rough seas. Others were attached to huge booms for taking on supplies. The old steel cable operated booms looked like something from an old war movie. The bridge of the ship looked modern enough with the standard squared off line of bridge windows running its length. Behind the windows you could see the original second level of the superstructure. The bridge had been rounded in front when it was first built. The squared off front façade was probably added during one of the re-commissioning make overs.

Two old style navigation radars were mounted to the top. They appeared oversized for the small ship, but it felt good to see them. If they worked at least the Reclaimer was not going to get lost underway. Between the two radars was a huge spotlight. The largest I had ever seen. This thing was the diameter of a fire department light, but twice as deep. I could only imagine the beam that it created.

I walked over to the guard's hut with my bag dragging behind me to sign in.

"Hello?" I said as I looked inside the old and leaning aluminum security hut. It offered about two square feet of standing room inside. The windows were plexiglass with breaks running across them. Several sheets of paper were taped to the windows and walls inside the hut. "Hello?" I said again.

Inside a sailor in blue dungarees was passed out on an old gray metal military chair that leaned up against one wall of the hut. It threatened to take the whole thing down with the weight of the sailor, not that this would have been a major loss. The sailor's steel toe black boots were up on the small aluminum shelf inside the hut. A black phone from the Korean War era sat on one end of the shelf as well. The sailor never moved.

I walked around the security hut and stood inside the Alpha Docks drive way. The yard was small with enough room for about four salvage vessels. The Reclaimer was docked at the pier in front and several work boats were moored around the base; fifty foot boats, larger ones as well. A long gray ship-looking thing sat at the far pier. It had a bow that looked like a sea going vessel, but no identifiable bridge to operate it from. Weird.

The whole base was left in the same condition it had been for decades. Very little time or effort was put into keeping up the buildings or piers. The metal buildings were rusted and needed repainting. The cement piers had stacks of steel cables and metal ship's anchor chain on them. Some stretched out and others twisted into piles. Metal, fifty gallon barrels were stacked around the Alpha Dock grounds and old yellow fork lifts were parked wherever they were last used.

The sun was beating down on the cement pier and the main road of the base. I decided to bypass the security sign in and just walk up to the ship and report in. The Reclaimer had a long metal gang way attached to its side giving access from the pier. I could not see anyone on board as the sun was shining past the main mast of the vessel and into my eyes. I made my way to the gang way, tossed my sea bag onto my back and walked up.

I held on tight to the rails as the gang way shook and rattled. It was barely held together with aluminum bolts and rope. I hoped it would keep together long enough for me to get my bag onto the ship. At that point I could grab on to the ship with both hands as the gang way crumbled behind me.

From the gang way I could see up and down the port side of the Reclaimer. Gallon cans of gray and white paint were set on the decks with brushes stuck in them. Rags were draped over rails and unidentifiable ships equipment to prevent paint splatter. I could now make out a few sailors in green and blue coveralls painting here and there. The sound of metal grinders came from around the far side of the ship. There also came what sounded like an air pressure hose bursting.

Once on board the Reclaimer I surveyed the quarterdeck. An old wooden podium sat facing the gang way I had traversed. There were no signs or plaques on the quarterdeck as are often seen on warships. Just the podium and a few cardboard boxes full of metal cans, perhaps paint or maybe food supplies for the mess decks.

The quarterdeck was filled with pipes and cables running all directions along the bulkheads. The overhang that covered the quarterdeck area, and provided a second level above, was peeling paint and showing some rust. Two old light housings with yellow bulbs inside were turned on, but were too dirty and paint covered to provide any real light in the shaded quarterdeck area.

I did not see anyone manning the quarterdeck so I wandered forward along the port side. Some yelling caught my ear from over the side. I held the railing and leaned over to see what was going on. Between the bow and pier were two sailors in green coveralls covered with paint splashes of many colors; gray, black, white and orange. They were balancing on a small wooden row boat as they painted the ship with long poles and brush attachments. They were yelling at each other to keep the boat still as they tried to complete the job.

"Can I help you?" A voice called from behind me. I turned around and saw a young man in blue dungarees seated on a wooden stool behind the podium on the quarterdeck. I did not see him behind there when I first came on board. I walked back to him and the quarterdeck. He was fiddling with a small transistor radio behind the podium. The radio crackled and hummed as he tried to find a station. Without looking back up at me he asked again, "Can I help you find someone?"

"Uh..." I answered. I looked down at him. His uniform was one step up from rags. His blue ballcap was torn and frayed at the edges revealing the yellow foam under the blue brim covering. It was stenciled USS Reclaimer ARS 42. He wore a green belt around his waste with an old Vietnam era pistol holder attached to it. Inside I could see the butt end of a .45 caliber handgun. "I'm checking into the command, from dive school."

"Yeah?" That made him look up at me. He was unshaved and needed a good shower as well. His hair stuck out in all directions from under the ball cap. He stood up and smiled at me, taking a sip of coffee from a cup he had under the podium. "Checking in, eh? God help ya'."

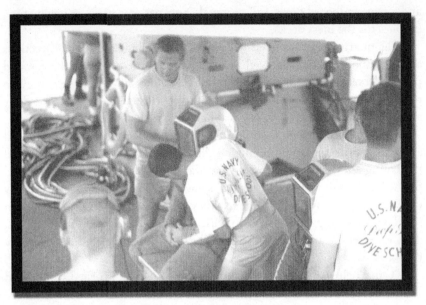

U.S. Navy deep sea diver candidates at Pearl Harbor, Hawaii prepare divers for a training dive using the Mark 12 dive suit and helmet. Candidates are shown on board the dive barge operated by the Ford Island dive school for open ocean training.

The author operating the communication gear or "comm set" during an open ocean training dive.

Dive station tenders gear divers with the Mark 12 deep diving suit on the shore line of Pearl Harbor's Ford Island dive school facility. In the background the "grinder" physical training area can be seen.

Open ocean SCUBA training off the coast of Honolulu, Hawaii.

Open ocean SCUBA training. Divers prepare to descend along a weighted line with bright float attached.

Divers team up into pairs of two called "buddy teams" for SCUBA operations.

The Ford Island dive school flatbed truck that doubled as a personnel carrier for trips into Waikiki on the weekends.

The balanced diet of a dive school candidate.

Carbohydrate loading for the physical training the next day.

Deep sea dive school class 9010-2C takes a break from Mark 12 dive station for a quick photo. Pearl Harbor shipyard is visible in the background.

The author in the Mark 12 dive suit and helmet. Notice the air flow controls on the sides of the helmet and microphone seen inside.

A diver in Mark 12 gear descends into the ocean on a dive station ladder. The dive school instructor is seen observing the diver and dive station operations.

Chapter 4.

Haze Gray and Underway.

The young man at the quarterdeck had a familiar east coast accent, probably New Jersey or New York. Having been stationed in Philadelphia with my father I knew the accent well. He reached out his hand to shake.

"Welcome dude." He said. "Grab your bag and let's check you into the dive locker." He introduced himself as Halcola, an east coast Italian kid about twenty years old.

I grabbed my sea bag and followed him into the ship. The Reclaimer's doors were small and oval in shape. They were the traditional water tight doors one would see in old movies about the navy. This ship was a sailing museum of salvage navy history.

The inside of the ship was tight. My guide and I squeezed through doorways and down thin ladder wells. The angle of the steps on board were a dead 45 degrees and I figured they would be dangerous when underway. Bars to act as hand holds were everywhere. We hugged the bulkheads to allow others to pass and ducked through every passage as the overheads were low. People were smaller in the 1940's and the ships were not designed to have been in service for sixty years.

The ship's interior was lit by florescent tubes and standard bulbs housed in a variety of plastic and glass housings. Nothing on the ship matched as lights and other features were changed out or repaired over the decades. The bulkheads and overheads were loaded with thousands of cables running to and fro. Layers of paint and insulation covered the various pipes and electrical equipment attached to the ship. The floors were mostly old tile with years worth of wax and paint drippings on them. Each area we entered had different flooring.

"Throw your bag in here. This is where you guys bunk, with the deck division." My guide told me. He opened a gray door that led into a cramped berthing space. Bunks were stacked three high and were too close to even sit up inside. The bunks were covered with towels, blankets and dirty clothes that stank horribly. There had to be bunks for thirty people in this tight space. The bunk room was barely the size of a passenger van! Yet, thirty sailors called this space home. I found an empty bunk near one end of the room and placed my sea bag on it. I took a mesh sack full of smelly clothes off of my new bunk and hung it from one of the bulkheads.

Outside the deck division bunk room Halcola showed me the adjoining head (bathroom) and showers. The head did not have room for thirty guys to use effectively. Perhaps three. Most of the ship's head was stainless steel which would make it easy to hose down inside. The smell of bleach told me that someone had cleaned it that morning. The walls were covered with stainless steel as well and dripped with water from the morning wash down. The head looked like a prison bathroom.

Halcola walked me through the ship from bow to stern. He pointed out the Chief Petty Officer's bunk area and the mess decks. The mess decks were big enough to hold about forty guys. I would soon find out that it was the largest open space in the ship and doubled as a TV room and card game parlor while underway.

All the hallways were tight and several sailors passing by turned to let us through. I shook hands and said hello as I went. Halcola pointed out various spaces, like the engineering office and the electrician's shack. Each space was the size of a medium closet. Inside they were crammed with books, manuals, log sheets and grease pencil chart boards posted on the bulkheads. As always there were loads of cables running along the overheads. The Reclaimer had to fit all the necessary ship's divisions and departments into the skin of the vessel. There was not enough room for comfort. Deck division, engineering, administration, and everything else had just enough room for a few people to sit and perhaps a work desk. Other than that the spaces on board were filled with the needed equipment to keep the ship running.

I was shown the ladders leading down into the actual engine rooms. The smell of oil and diesel fuel rose from these lower spaces and I could hear the sounds of tools rattling and grinding below. There was a sense of constant upkeep on this ship. Every division was working hard to maintain the vessel's integrity and seaworthiness. Two engineers carried buckets and tool pouches past me and down the stairs into the engine room.

As the Reclaimer was not very long, we soon reached the aft deck area just past the engineering spaces. An ARS has a primary salvage and ship rescue mission so the aft work deck area, the fantail, was full of steel chains, heavy ship's lines and towing equipment. Salvage vessels of the Reclaimer's class were designed to tow ships that were damaged in battle out of danger. For that reason the fantail had a heavy tow machine, a long coil of steel cable and a set of "H-bits", huge mounts to tie down a ship's line if they needed a tow, in the shape of the letter H.

What looked like the remnants of a dive station was visible on the fantail as well. Two color coded diving umbilical cords were coiled on the deck and a steel chair to seat a diver in full gear were still remaining. Perhaps they were just finishing a repair of their own ship or a training exercise. I could not tell.

On the fantail several sailors were taking a break from their various duties to soak up some sunlight. I shook more hands and introduced myself. Their coveralls were coated with grease and paint which appeared to be the norm onboard. They drank cola and coffee from the mess decks while a few smoked cigarettes. The crew was a good cross section of America. East coast, west coast, mid-western boys and southern red-necks. Inner-city African-Americans worked side by side with white farm boys. Race was not an issue of division here, the crew counted on each other like a family.

As the Reclaimer was stationed in Hawaii, some Polynesian and Hawaiian sailors had requested to be stationed on board instead of being sent to the mainland United States naval bases or ships. They were able to do their sea time here and go home every night to their families.

In all, the crew was a good group. This was a hard duty station so everyone tried to make the best of it. Humor, bad coffee and alcohol numbed reality and made a two year stint bearable.

Back inside the ship Halcola led me to the ladder-well leading to the aft engineering spaces. "Hey," He said, "I have to get back top side, so, just go down here and walk aft. The dive locker is back there. You will see the door. Just keep walking aft." With that he turned to go.

I looked down the stairs and into the abyss. The aft engine spaces were dark and smelled of burnt oil. The flicker of bright light foretold that a team of welders were working below. The noise of running generators emanated from the space below with a loud rumble. It looked foreboding and I turned to ask Halcola a question, but he was already gone.

I held onto the rails and descended to the next deck down. The decks were steel grates bolted to the various bulkheads (walls) and supports. I could see through the grates to the engines and motors running below. Engine and motor repair groups were working both on my level and the one below. They were shouting over the generator noise and waving their arms to send messages.

I walked aft through the space and around equipment mounted to the deck plating. Water pumps, air pressure flasks, never ending cables and pipes filled the area. The space was dark as only a few bulbs glowed from sockets hung above the machinery. Steam was rising from the level below and passed through the steel grating. The drifting steam rose into the air around me and smelled of stale water.

I could barely make out the water tight door leading to the dive locker in the dim light. Through the steam and hanging cables I could make out the lettering on the locker door. The steel, water tight door was painted with a "mark 5" dive helmet that seemed right at place on this ship where the mark 5 stood as the primary dive rig for decades no doubt. I pulled up on the door's release bar and opened it. The water tight seal and hinges creaked and groaned as the door swung open.

I closed the door behind me shutting out the noise and steam of the engine space. The dive locker door led to a hallway, well lit with a terracotta colored steel floor and white walls. There were three doors leading from the hallway. One, another water tight door, led aft while the other two doors, both wood and aluminum framed, led port and starboard of the hallway. The door leading to starboard was labeled "gear locker." The door leading to port was labeled "Master Diver" so I figured this was a good place to check in.

I had better explain something here.

The Navy has various levels of salvage divers based upon a diver's knowledge and experience. As a diver goes through their career, divers are sent to the next level of training and return to the fleet more capable than before.

First and foremost a young sailor can expect to attend second class dive school and be assigned to a dive command as a worker. Second class divers perform the maintenance and operation of the dive station, equipment and hyper baric chambers. Second class divers are the labor force and worker bees of the diving navy. Second class divers are well trained in SCUBA and hard helmet diving using common air.

After working in the fleet for a few years as a second class diver (usually two or more years) a diver can request to be sent to first class diver school in Panama City, Florida. First class training is based upon developing a supervisor on the dive station. First class divers take turns running dive stations and reacting to simulated medical emergencies. First class divers also begin to work with mixed air or Helium/Oxygen equipment. Helium/Oxygen diving allows for dives deeper than two hundred feet giving the navy a much wider field of operation for salvage and rescue work.

Sailors can remain first class divers for the rest of their careers if they choose. Divers who are promoted in rank keep their first class diver status. A diver can be sent to a variety of commands as a first class diver so it does not limit their options.

Navy corpsmen (medical personnel) are able to attend both second and first class school. Corpsmen then qualify as diving medical technicians. Diving medical technicians complete a long and tough academic program alongside the two diving schools. Once In the fleet, diving medical technicians are a valuable part of the dive command and are present on any mixed gas or deep dive. Often diving medical technichans will supervise medical treatments in the hyper-baric recompression chamber and actually work inside the chamber with the injured diver. Diving medical technicians are well respected in the fleet and other divers treat them good. Divers know the diving medical tech may save their ass in the future.

When navy officers decide to go for a new challenge they can also join the diving navy. Dive officers attend first class school in Panama City, Florida and focus on supervisory dive work. Diving officers are assigned to tenders and salvage vessels as their sea going commands. The commanding officer of any ARS must be a qualified diving officer to understand and relate to the dive side of the ship's duties.

The brave few who have worked as first class divers in the fleet for years choose to go on to saturation diver training, also in Panama City, Florida. Saturation divers are a secretive and well respected group of divers who use unusual gasses and experimental dive rigs to go thousands of feet under the water. Saturation divers live and work at those depths for days or weeks before slowly returning to the surface.

Note: I have a good friend from Hawaii who chose this path in his diving career. He is one of the finest people I know and he is still in the service. I have no idea what he does on a day to day basis in the "special projects" unit, but I just hope he makes it to retirement safe and comes home to the islands.

At every dive command there are a variety of well trained divers each playing an important role on dive station. Dive officers supervise and plan operational movements as first class divers give commands to set up dive station and "suit up." Second class divers lay out hundreds of feet of umbilical cords for the divers and start to gear up themselves for the days work.

Everyone has a position. Everyone knows what they are accountable for. At the same time, everyone knows who is overall responsible for the dive station, the job, the divers, dive officers, safety, emergencies and every damn thing else…the master diver.

In the dive navy there are a select few Chief Petty Officers, first class divers all, who accept a career path that may possibly hold more responsibility and accountability than anyone else in the Navy save the poor bastards who run nuclear reactors on submarines. These divers choose to become a Master Diver. While master divers are enlisted and not officers, the navy bestows ultimate responsibility for what takes place on a deep sea diving operation in the master diver's hands. No excuses, no pointing fingers, if the stuff hit's the fan during a deep salvage or rescue operation, one individual will be standing before a panel of admirals to find out what happened, the master diver.

A master diver does not receive a significant pay increases or even advancement guarantees as most master divers are often master chief petty officers already and are at the top of the enlisted rank levels. The lives of a hundred sailors can be in a master diver's hands as they stand back and survey the dive station. A master diver will constantly ask themselves - are the supervisors aware of the time the divers have been down; are the officers aware of what stage this operation is in and where it will go next; are the divers alright or has it been too long since they checked in with the supervisor? Every possible scenario is running through a master diver's head and at the same time the master diver appears calm, collected and clear minded.

A diver must have years of diving and salvage experience to become a candidate for master diver. There is also an emphasis on technical diving operations, emergencies a candidate has dealt with in their career, complicated salvage projects they have supervised and a proven track record of leadership. A diver enters the master diver training program at the top of the game. After qualification, a master diver is capable of handling the most severe, dive-related emergencies and outlandish scenarios the Panama City, Florida instructors can throw at them.

A master diver will probably have a few decades of navy experience under their belt and have served in a war or two. I will never forget how whenever a situation went bad on dive station, regardless of the number of supervisors and dive officers on station standing around with charts, graphs and stopwatches around their necks, everyone still turned and looked at the old man with the cup of coffee off to the far end of the fantail. The master diver. If the master diver had to step in and take the watches from the supervisor, it meant the job was over and the mission was now to get two deep sea divers on station alive…period.

Master divers set the tone for any dive locker. If a master diver was gruff and work oriented, the locker followed suit. If the master diver liked attention, the command would be doing "dog and pony" shows for the local television station. It all revolved around this one individual. A diver didn't have to impress the master diver to get ahead, just do the job and don't screw up. I would have taken captain's mast well before I stood in front of my master diver for failure to do my duty in any way.

One more thing, there is another saying in the dive navy, "your first master diver molds you." It is very true. The command a diver goes to out of second class dive school and the master diver that runs that command's dive locker will play a role in a diver's personality and work habits for the rest of their life! After all, a new diver is about 19 years old when they get to their first command. The master diver will play a key aspect in how a young diver views the world around them for life. Thank god for this. My first master diver figured the world could throw anything it wanted to at him and he would knock it right back on its ass. Following suit, I have been the same way ever since.

This was the day I met Master Chief Boatswains Mate / Master Diver Edward Starkey.

I slowly opened the door to the master diver's office and it creaked with the sound of thirty year old spring hinges. The light was off inside so I figured the master diver must have been out for the day. I decided to leave a note about my arrival and try back after lunch. The room inside was small and the florescent lights flickered when I clicked them on. They began to glow with a dim white light exposing the rest of the small office that I could not see from the hall lights behind me.

Leaning back on an old, gray, steel, military chair was a huge man… huge. The man was about three hundred pounds wearing a khaki colored jump suit with the front zipper zipped down all the way to the belly button. He had a big belly but a normal sized upper body and legs. The sun burn on his chest and stomach showed he kept his zipper down most of the time to accommodate. He had short dark hair and no shave. No neck, his huge head just attached to his shoulders. His black cowboy boots were visible because of his position leaning back. The blue ship's ball cap sitting on the desk next to him had a large, gold and distinct dive pin affixed to it. Master diver. Oh, hell.

The man snored once or twice. When the door behind me came to a close with a spring loaded, Thwack, the mountain of a man let out a sharp snort. I stood motionless and just stared at him. He was not asleep anymore, but he did not move.

Then with slow and deliberate movements the master diver opened one eye and let it roll around to the side to meet mine. He did not speak right away, but just looked at me with that one eye. At last he opened his mouth on one side to speak.

"You got two choices, son. Turn off that light or wish you did." He stayed in his leaning back position and gave me that one-eye-look. His hands were folded just below his massive belly.

"Uh...Sorry." I quickly said and grabbed the door. As I retreated from the office I shut off the light.

"Wait!" The man shouted at me from the darkness.

I turned around and slowly peered back into the room, one arm holding open the door for a fast escape if need be. "Sir?" I said quietly, as if not to disturb him any further.

"Don't call me sir, <god damn it>. Get me something from the mess decks." He snorted at me.

"Aye, master diver." I said and left for the engine room and mess decks above at once. I had no idea what they would have to eat if it was not lunch time yet, but I would find something. Damn! The master diver had it out for me already and he did not even know who I was yet. I was screwed.

I introduced myself to the mess specialists on board. The cooks. The mess specialists understood my dilemma and threw some meat and bread together into a makeshift sandwich. I had the Reclaimer's cooks make a few more and I carried them back down into the sub-levels of the ship. Back to the dive locker.

Master diver Starkey and I sat in his office, he on his chair and me on the floor, and ate sandwiches as I introduced myself. Starkey was not a mean person nor did he have it out for anyone. Master Diver Ed Starkey was a true hard ass. He talked loud and threw people around when they were lazy, but he just wanted the job done and done right. Starkey explained to me his work ethics and philosophies. The master diver expected to get work done first so that the divers could barbeque and have a few drinks at the end of the day. Good plan, I figured. Master diver Starkey and I were from very different backgrounds, but we shared the idea that hard work kept the officers happy. It the officers were off the dive locker's back everything went smooth.

Master diver Starkey had a hard time pronouncing names in general, but mine was particularly hard. Starkey would bellow out "La-Hoy-a <god damn> ." Master diver Starkey spoke with fast and loud bursts followed by whispers of hard to understand end statements. Usually obscenities, but sometimes just words.

Starkey had seen years of hard labor in the dive navy; Vietnam, years of salvage boat tours and, of course, the mark 5 rig.

As Starkey and I talked the other divers on board wandered through. The divers introduced themselves and their backgrounds. The divers wanted to know where I went to dive school. I told them Ford Island, right there in Pearl Harbor, Hawaii.

Ford Island was often referred to as "vacation dive school" in the fleet. The first thing a new diver had to do when they arrived at their first command from Ford Island was to prove they could work and not just play volley ball.

The Reclaimer's dive locker was a mix of personalities. The first class divers who ran the locker under master diver Starkey had good experience in salvage and diving operations. Some of the Reclaimer's first class divers were attached to deck department instead of the dive locker, but during diving operations all of the Reclaimer's divers worked together to perform the dive job.

There were other second class divers I would work with on board. McNamara and I clicked as friends early as we both had a good sense of humor and did not take the Navy too seriously. Baxter was well educated and a good outdoorsman. Together, with Gordon when he would later check in, the second class divers on board made up the core of the ships locker and dive team.

Master diver Starkey wanted me to go with the other divers and learn what the dive locker encompassed. Starkey would meet up with me later to discuss my work duties and my areas of responsibility.

I was surprised to hear that I would be in charge of salvage gear and diving rigs already. I was just out of school and figured I would be someone's assistant for awhile. There just were not enough divers on board for that. The Reclaimer had about six in the locker itself, all attached to deck division while underway, and a few more divers worked their rates as engineers. Everyone had responsibilities and everyone stayed busy.

Divers had to repair and upkeep dive gear and salvage equipment on top of their duties to deck or engineering departments. Working for deck division meant long hours painting, grinding and operating the ship's heavy gear on the forward and after deck areas. This was the hard and dangerous work that "junk boats" were infamous for.

Below decks, through the watertight door that led past the master diver's office, was the "yellow gear." Yellow gear was the nick name given to the salvage pumps and hydraulic machinery that the Reclaimer carried in its storage spaces. Yellow gear was painted bright yellow and fell under the dive locker's responsibilities. Divers repaired, operated and moved that heavy damn gear around almost every day. The work was miserable, but yellow gear was a key part of what a salvage ship was built for.

As I was to become best friend and enemy to this gear, let me explain it further. Yellow gear consisted of huge water pumps, with inlet and outlet pipes of about twelve inches. Attached were huge diesel motors to pump thousands of gallons per hour through the machine. A dive team, during a rescue or salvage operation, could pump out a sinking vessel and keep the ship afloat even if it had a direct hit under the waterline from a five inch shell. These "salvage" pumps weighed as much as a truck and moving them around in a tight compartment, underway, while taking major rolls to port and starboard could kill someone. Moving and manipulating this gear took full blood, sweat and bruises.

The bulkheads around the yellow gear were, of course, steel and so was the gear itself. If the master diver wanted the hydraulic tow machines drug up from the salvage gear spaces, a diver knew someone was going to get pinned between gear and a steel bulkhead some how that day. Now add in the problem of being at sea and taking heavy waves, which is usually the condition that the ocean is in when the Reclaimer is sent to rescue a stricken ship. Now divers need to have eyes behind their back to not get killed.

Moving and operating yellow gear would constitute a million dollar a day contract for a civilian company. The danger levels and expertise warranted it. In the Navy, the average second class diver was paid about three hundred dollars a week to do it. As always, there were no scapegoats if things went wrong and a machine exploded or crushed someone. The master diver was in charge of any salvage operation. Even the captain of a salvage vessel would stand by and release operational command to the master diver if a rescue situation warranted a major draw out of yellow gear. It was not about rank, it was about keeping divers alive.

Salvage and rescue was the bulk of a diver's above water job while stationed on an ARS type vessel. Make no mistake, and ARS like the Reclaimer carried SCUBA, Mark 12 systems with full suits and thousands of feet of umbilical cord in order to sustain a deep diving operation for weeks if need be. Yet, most jobs the Reclaimer was called out for revolved around drifting, sinking or burning ships at sea. If the damn thing sunk already, the divers on board could raise it, sure, we just wouldn't have to get there as fast, I guess.

Salvage sailors were always exposed to one insane dangerous job after another. Rescues at sea, tows in rough waters, huge ship board fires, the Reclaimer was were sent to them all. Once there, divers were assigned to any direct contact position that would arise in the rescue operation. I figured this out after I left the Reclaimer two years later. Any time that Reclaimer sailors needed to board or make contact with an object that posed a threat to that sailors life, one of the dive locker members would be geared up and ordered out. It was humorous to think about, after I got off the ship.

I was introduced to the upkeep and operational ideas of each piece of gear in the salvage/diving spaces. There were several kinds of yellow gear and lockers full of strange hooks, hinges, pins, chains and steel pry bars. Everything a dive team may possibly need while underway to fulfill a mission. If the Reclaimer did not have it, the machinists on boards were well versed in building any odd-ball device that master diver Starkey would tell them to. The whole vessel was a lean and rough riding rescue machine. When the ship was sent out, everyone worked as team to stay alive and get the job done.

There is a bond between sailors who have pulled a two year tour on an ARS. Many have worked on larger more modern war ships with open spaces and comfortable bunk rooms. It can be a shock when a seasoned sailor walks onboard a world war two ship that has hallways wide enough for one person and barely enough room between bunks to hold a book in front of their face. Salvage ships are hard duty to pull.

For that reason ARS sailors had to keep our spirits up with practical jokes and thick skin. Sailors tried hard not to fight with each other and respect each other's privacy whenever possible. Often, it just was not possible. The Reclaimer had about a hundred sailors crammed into a ship just over two hundred feet long. Most of the ship was storage and machinery spaces.

It was not uncommon to find sailors sleeping on the outside decks while at sea trying to get some air or in the bellow decks machinery spaces. Only a salvage ship sailor could sleep on a running diesel engine about the size of a school bus. Just give a salvage sailor a pair of ear protectors and a ball cap to cover their eyes and they could sleep through an earthquake. ARS sailors just got used to a miserable life style.

Salvage ships did not get much respect from the rest of the fleet. Cruisers and carriers took precedence well over our tub when it came to operational readiness spending and upkeep. The Reclaimer was expected to do its missions with what it had. No excuses. Salvage ship captains were masters of improvisation. A captain had to think fast to stay afloat when they were operating a 1940's ship.

A good example was during a Pacific Ocean crossing, from Honolulu, Hawaii to San Diego, California. Underway the Reclaimer took hard rolls as its hull was shaped much like that of a whale's underside. This shape made our draft shallow so the Reclaimer could get deeper into a river delta or coral bed to rescue a beached ship. With every roll the Reclaimer would groan under the strain. Old metal skins and rivets tried to hold her together as years of wear and tear had taken it's toll.

In deck department berthing, where I slept, my bunk was on the other side of the ship's steel skin from the main anchor. The anchor would swing out with every roll to Port and come crashing back into the side of the ship when the Reclaimer rolled back to Starboard. It was an almost amusing miserable situation. I tried to tell myself that the ship's rolls were like a cradle rocking me to sleep, but I could not rationalize that damn multi-ton anchor away.

Finally, I was roused from my poor excuse for slumber to take "sound and security" watch. Sound and security is a standard watch that all navy vessels used. One sailor would walk the ship from bow to stern every hour and report back to the bridge that all was well. On the way the sailor would check deep spaces for possible signs of leaking. On the Reclaimer, there was leaking all the time, so I would make sure that the on board pumps were keeping up with the water. Now, isn't that nice?

I took the green belt from the current watchman and he crawled into his bunk. The sailor was so tired from the days work and the long watch that he did not even take off his coveralls and boots. Wearing only boxer shorts, I took the log book and belt under my arm and stumbled around looking for my coveralls. I put them on as I wandered up to the bridge to check in.

The midnight watch was miserable on any ship unless the sailors were allowed to sleep during the day time work hours. Radio operators and other tech rates could afford this luxury. Engineers and divers worked a full day on the Reclaimer and then stood midnight watch with no whining allowed.

After checking in I strapped the belt around my waste, a green rag dangling from it to wipe water and oil drips as I wandered the ship for an hour. I made my way to the mess decks for a hot cup of coffee and grabbed a second for the poor bastard watching the Reclaimer's engineering panel below. The engineering watch was generally an electrician sitting at the engine department's main operation panel below decks in the after engine space. This sailor controlled the speed of the engines and the ships generators.

I handed the mid-watch engineer the cup of coffee and sat next to him. It was so damn loud in that engine space that the two of us could not really talk to each other. The roar of pumps, generators and motors filled the space with loud noises. If I did not have ear protection I would have gone crazy down there. I nodded hello to the duty electrician and jotted notes into the sound and security watch log.

Just then we both heard a loud clanging from the engine space below us. Remember that I told you the after engine spaces were separated with steel grates and not full steel decks. For that reason the engineers who were in the lower spaces could rap on a support beam with a pipe wrench to get someone's attention on the level above them. It was crude, but it was the way engineers communicated on the Reclaimer in those spaces from the day the ship hit the water in World War Two. Some things do not have to be changed as they just work.

The duty electrician and I looked bellow us and into the lower engine space. One of the engineers on mid watch below was pointing to me and waving his arm to say "get down here, now!" Damn, just what I needed, some stinking problem. I just wanted to sit for a while and rest my bones before I walked around the boat. Now something was up.

The way things work on a ship is that a sailor does not tell anyone above them in rank about a problem unless they absolutely can not deal with it themselves. The idea was that enlisted sailors fixed a problem first and told their Chief Petty Officers about it as a last resort. If the Chief realized it was going to take more than a day to fix the problem they told the department head officer. If the officer figured that it may take more than a week to repair, or that the ship was in danger because of it, they would report it to the Executive Officer (XO), the second in command of the ship. Finnaly, if the problem involved the need of off-ship services and may bring the fleet commander's attention to the ship, the XO would take it to the Commanding Officer (CO).

This incident would become a good example of that operational theory. I walked down the ladder into the lower engine room and held up my arms to the mid watch engineer as if to say "well, what the hell is up?" The mid-watch engineer, covered in grease and oil stains from head to toe, pointed down to the steel hull that could be seen below a metal grate used as a walk way between two pieces of running machinery. The hull was painted terracotta, clean, as if it had been painted by the engine department just before the Reclaimer got underway.

I walked over to the exposed hull plating, kneeled down and looked far under one of the running generators bolted to the hull. There, about an arm's length from the walk way grating, was a small hole that had rusted its way through the forty plus year old hull and was slowly leaking water into the ship's bilge. The leaking hole was about a half an inch in diameter and bubbled water into the lower engine room bilges at a rate of about a few gallons per hour. Not bad and not unusual for the Reclaimer, but in need of plugging as to not to draw the attention of the engineering Chief Petty Officer tomorrow morning.

I laughed about the hole in the hull along with the engineer. The poor Reclaimer was trying its best to keep on running, but years of hard work had thinned the ship's hull and bent its ribs. The engineers would weld a patch onto it when the Recalimer pulled into San Diego. Until then I pointed over to a metal box welded onto one of the engine space's bulkheads. The box was full of small, medium and large wooden plugs for emergency repairs. The plugs were shaped like cones and were hammered into place with a wooden mallet next to the box.

The engineer brought me a small plug and the mallet. The plug was about three inches at the wide end and would plug the small hole in the hull fine until the Reclaimer arrived in port. I reached far under the running generator and with all my arm strength, in this awkward position, I pushed the wooden plug into place. The hole was small so it did not apply much water pressure against the plug. The hole did not leak. With the same arm I took the wooden mallet by the handle and slowly reached under again to give the wooden plug a few taps.

There was not much swing room under the generator so I planned to just tap the plug several times to seal the hole. The position I was in made it difficult to hit the target and I worked slowly so as not to knock the plug out all together. With the engineer next to me looking under the generator, I rose up the mallet and brought it down with all the strength I could get from my over extended arm. The mallet came down squarely onto the plug and pushed it right through the hull and into the ocean below. The force of the blow also took about four inches of thin, rusted hull with it. Hell, the damn mallet dropped out the hole as well!

There was now a solid six inch gushing hole in the hull of the Reclaimer and the ship was about a hundred friggin' miles from any port. Shocked, I looked back over my shoulder at the engineer behind me. His face was stuck in a frightened position, eyes wide and mouth open full. It was to loud to hear him in the engine room, but I knew the engineer was yelling obsenities at the situation. The two of us got up and ran for the electrician sitting at the engine panel watch.

Behind us the aft engine room bilge was filling up as seawater poured into the space at a high rate.

The electrician mid watch was leaning back on his chair and staring at the little black generator gauges on the engine panel waver back and forth. The gauges would hypnotize a sailor if stared at like that. For that reason the electrician did not even notice the engineer and I climbing our way up the ladder yelling bloody murder and waving our arms. When I was standing over the electrician he woke up from his fixed gaze with a startle.

The mid-watch electrician could not hear me, but he knew I was freaking out about something bad. I pointed to the black phone on the bulkhead and pointed upwards as if to say I needed to send a message to the bridge. The electrician spun the ringer and the bridge watchman answered via a huge electric bull horn mounted in the engineering panel room.

"Bridge," The booming voice spoke out into the engine space. I took the phone handle from the panel watch and yelled in to it.

"Sounding and security, bridge, we have a flooding situation here! Aft engine room!" I shouted. The bull horn was silent for a while. I figured the guy on the bridge mid watch was thinking the same thing I was when the engineer alerted me. Damn!

"Officer of the watch here. Engine room, say again. What is your situation?" The problem was rolling uphill fast as the mid-watch on the bridge had given the information to the bridge officer. I knew it was going to roll back down just as fast.

I yelled back into the phones, "Flooding, sir! Aft engine room! Major flooding into the aft engine room!"

The horn was silent again. I could see the bridge officer's face in my mind. The young liutenant was pissed and knew he had to pull the alarm for this. I was the sound and security watch for Christ's sake! If I called the bridge with an emergency, it meant there was a real emergency. That was my job!

With out a return message from the bridge the Reclaimer's general alarm began to sound throughout the entire ship. When the crew hears that alarm go off and they wake up in the middle of the dark night, realizing that the ship is between Hawaii and California somewhere in the Pacific, the crew will get up quick. The whole ship was awake and gearing up for anything. General alarm is a miserable way to wake up the crew. The general alarm was the wrong way to wake up the captain. There was, however, no time in an emergency for anything else.

Engine room sailors clamored down the ladder wells and into the space. The crew was all geared up for fires and damage control. Standing in the aft engine space they were yelling at me for answers. Of all places to be. I stood there yelling back at the engineers and pointing at the water flooding in.

Engine department supervisors and Chief Petty Officers came down next and began to bark orders at those standing around. Engineers ran to their posts and prepared damage control gear. Others surveyed the hull with the Chiefs and yelled ideas at each other. After a few minutes everyone shot to their feet and backed away from the damaged hull. The crew made room as the captain, pissed off and staring with a look that could kill, stepped down the ladder and into the space.

The Chiefs pointed to the hull break and water poring in and yelled information into the captain's ear. The engine rooms were very loud and the noise of emergency gear being drug down the ladders made it even worse. The captain nodded as the various Chiefs gave their reports and recommendations.

The ladder behind the captain made a loud clang as a huge boot hit the first metal step. The captain and chiefs turned as Master Diver Starkey, also awoken by the general alarm, stepped heavy down the stairs cursing into the loud engine room with inaudible shouts. Starkey did not wear the usual general alarm protective gear, just his usual khaki coveralls with the zipper down to his boxer shorts. The master diver held a ship's fire-helmet in one hand that someone above must have handed to him.

The captain and Starkey yelled ideas back and forth for a while as the engine room emergency pumps were turned on full blast. The water levels did not noticeably go down or even slow down. Starkey yelled out to the engine room watchman who had noticed the leaking in the first place. The watchman turned and pointed to me. Starkey looked past the engine room workers shuffling about and saw me standing in my coveralls and green sounding and security belt. The master diver held one hand up to his forehead and drug it down over his face and mouth cursing again.

Starkey waved over to me to follow him. The two of us went back up the engine room ladder and continued to the main deck level. Once out of the noise Starkey yelled to the other divers who had already heard the news of the flooding through the ship's grape vine and were laying out hoses to set up additional pumps. Starkey barked for the divers to set up two yellow gear pumps to help the ship's fixed bilge pumps expel the seawater.

The Reclaimer came to a stop and bobbed back and forth, forward to aft in the open ocean. The bobbing motion made things worse for the dive team as we opened the large steel covers on the fantail that protected the yellow gear bellow. Divers took up various posts, operating the large boom that raised the yellow gear out and bellow decks unbolting the gear from their mounts. Lines were tied to the gear to steady them, in theory, as the boom raised each piece out. With the ship rolling around the pumps banged against the bulkheads and other equipment. Some of the divers got very close to being pinned between the yellow gear as they held the lines and tried ease the pumps out onto the fantail.

Hoses were attached and tied to the ship's sides to send seawater back overboard. Other hoses were unrolled to the lower decks and tied to the steel grates with the ends touching the bilge bottom. Divers secured the heavy pumps to the deck of the fantail with steel and nylon tie-downs and fired the diesel engines up. The combination of the ship's pumps and the yellow gear caught up with the flooding sea water and the levels in the engine room began to recede.

Miles from a port to get help in patching the hull, the captain told master diver Starkey that the dive team would have to apply a patch until the Reclaimer could get into San Diego for more permanent repairs. The idea was to either weld a steel plate over the hole or secure a rubber patch to it from the outside. The weight of the seawater on the hull would help seal the rubber into the hole and steel cables would be coiled around the fantail and under the ship to help hold the patch in place.

Now, remember, the time was about one in the morning now in the middle of the Pacific ocean. The Reclaimer is stopped and bobbing like a cork in the water. Salvage pumps were loudly sending seawater over the side and everyone was looking at Starkey to figure out how the hell we were going to get this tub to California. Starkey sipped coffee and started to bark orders again.

The dive locker sprung into action as the ship's divers set up dive station on our own fantail. Underwater welding gear and rods were set up as well. In about an hour the dive locker team was ready to go with both SCUBA and hard hat rigs on deck. Umbilical cords were coiled in figure eight fashion and three steel dive seats were brought up from below. Two for the work divers and one for the stand by.

The idea was to use SCUBA to identify the problems that would face the divers in the patch process. The use of steel plating or rubber would be decided at that time. Then the team would gear up the deep sea dive gear and go to work patching the hull.

Starkey talked to the divers as I donned SCUBA gear for the hull inspection. I was relieved from my watch to man dive station so I geared up first. I figured that any way I looked at it I was going to get some knocks from Starkey for this in the end so I had better volunteer first to fix the damn hole. Starkey leaned over me as I strapped on steel tanks and an inflatable vest.

"Measure that thing out. <damn La-hoy-a> I need to know how damn big it is." Starkey's deep and grumbled voice dictated to me. " What patch or whatever. <two in the morning, damn> Don't get hurt either! Captains pissed off already. So am I! <son of a...> use the dive lights and don't get fouled up on anything down there. Its dark as hell."

My buddy diver, also in SCUBA and I jumped into the black ocean, about two in the morning, and signaled the station divers that we were going below. The two of us had lines tied to our gear and held by the divers above to keep an eye on our position should we lose our direction in the zero visibility of the cold, dark water. With my flashlight in front of me I stayed as close to the hull as I could and went hand over hand to the point where the hole was supposed to be. Starkey had the engineers rap on the hull, lightly, to signal me as to the location. I thought to myself that between the loud clanging noise on the hull of the ship and the bright flashlight I was carrying I must be attracting every night roaming beast in the friggin' Pacific to my location. Great.

After some searching I found the hole. A steady flow of seawater into the hole was visible by the tiny debris and bubbles in the ocean getting sucked in. I could see it by my flashlight beam. Because of the thin hull in this area, the engineers decided not to try a larger plug on the hole. The captain must have feared opening a twelve inch gushing spout. That would have been interesting. The United Stated is not even at war with anyone and the news would report a Navy ship sinking in the Pacific Ocean. All crew saved by the Coast Guard. God help us.

I measured the hole with my hand and returned to Starkey above. On the surface I swam to where the master diver stood looking over the side. Starkey had his coffee in hand and a stern look on his face like he was pissed at the world. I explained the situation, the thin hull, the rust, the hole size and Starkey nodded his understanding. The master diver talked with the captain for awhile about the different patch ideas. Meanwhile my buddy and I bobbed in the water, lights off now, and looked around just waiting to see a fin coming at us or something.

The decision was made to use the rubber patch so the divers and deck department strapped long steel cables onto the fantail. Starkey said the hell with the Mark 12 rigs and had them broken down. The team would use SCUBA to lay the cables against the bottom of the hull and on both sides of the hole. A sheet of one inch thick rubber was cut and handed down to me in the water.

The square sheet of rubber covered the hole and was held in place by the two steel cables. The sea water pressure against the rubber patch held it snug just as planned and only a trickle of water made it past. The cables were tightened to hold while the ship was moving and the job was done.

The sky was just breaking daylight as the dive team shut down the yellow gear pumps and started to wash the fantail with fresh water hoses. The hole was patched well enough to get to San Diego and most of the crew were eating an early breakfast prepared in the mess decks. The divers broke down dive station and cleaned the last of the SCUBA gear to be stowed below. No one was seriously injured beyond the normal cuts and bruises that any job on an ARS would bring.

By mid morning the Reclaimer was underway for San Diego. The dive locker crew were passed out in the gear storage room below. Starkey was in his office asleep as well. I sat on the fantail drinking coffee with some of the other sailors and told them the story about the plug and wooden mallet. The crew members laughed and smoked cigarettes. I had made a hell of an impression on this crew already. A few months on board and I almost sank the damn ship.

Chapter 5.

Panama to Seattle.

The primary mission of the USS Reclaimer, when not involved in a rescue of some sort, was to tow vessels from port to port for logistical reasons. The Reclaimer saved the Navy and ultimately the taxpayers millions of dollars by not having to hire a civilian tug. Several months into my two year tour on the ship the Reclaimer was assigned to tow a decommissioned submarine to the sub's final resting place, the Seattle "mothball" ship yards.

The submarine the Reclaimer was scheduled to tow was stationed on the East coast of the United States, probably at Groton, Connecticut, and was being towed to the Panama Canal by another salvage vessel. The Reclaimer would make a long trip from Honolulu to the nation of Panama and the Panama Canal to meet up with the submarine on the Pacific coast side. In Panama the Reclaimer would relieve the other vessel from the tow and head north up the Pacific coastline towards Seattle.

Going to Panama was a surprise for Reclaimer crew. The ousting of Noriega as the dictator-like ex-president of Panama had just happened 30 days before our trip! Panama was still considered a hot zone for pro-Noriega factions. The Army Rangers and M-1 Tanks had torn through Panama City pummeling Noriega's loyal troops just a few weeks before the Reclaimer was to arrive for the tow. Oh... this would be fun.

Off I went for my first real cruise on the Reclaimer. As the ship left Honolulu the captain played "Panama" by Van Halen over the ship's main loudspeaker system. Playing a song over the loudspeaker was a positive gesture and helped to ease the pain of the men who were leaving their families behind for so long. It was an old navy tradition. At around 8 knots the Reclaimer would take a good twenty days or more to go from Hawaii to Panama.

Open ocean could leave an impression on a young sailor. No more so than when crossing on a small vessel. A sailor could feel their mortality on the open ocean when they were on a small ship. The captain may have had command of the vessel itself, but the captain still respected the ocean. A ship crosses the ocean at the pleasure of the water itself and the water can get angry fast.

When a ship the size of an aircraft carrier cruised through the oceans it had so much mass that a sailor on board may not even feel the effects of waves and currents. Carriers had a dozen support vessels with them as well which gave a feeling of "commanding the seas". Large ship sailors may have worked indoors for weeks without setting foot outside to look at the waves and feel the winds. These heavy and powerful war vessels would cut effortlessly through the seawater.

That is not how it felt on the Reclaimer. My tiny vessel would slowly make its way across the Pacific ocean. The Reclaimer would bob back and forth, side to side, at the will of the huge swells it encountered. The Reclaimer was designed with large and mostly flat propellers, "screws" in the Navy. These screws gave the Reclaimer little speed, but tremendous torque when pulling a heavy load.

The ship's crew would spend our off time on the "weather decks" or those that were exposed to the outside elements. The Reclaimer was designed with little open space inside the ship. The sailors would relax on the fantail or just behind the warm vents expelling hot air from the engine rooms. My favorite place was at the very top of the ship where the signalmen would stand watch. After my shift, on whatever watch I had been on, I would grab my CD player, books and something to eat and head for the top deck.

Open sea spread out from the Reclaimer in every direction. No support vessels were attached to our ship, no one. Just the Reclaimer rolling along with its familiar knocking noises from the engine room and the smell of gasoline in the air. I quietly read and listened to my music, lying down on the top deck and staring up at the clouds as they danced back and forth with the ships rolls.

One evening I stayed up late and talked to the signalman on duty. At night the signalmen on the top deck would use night vision goggles to search for drifting debris or derelict vessels that may have been missed by the Reclaimer's radars and posed a collision hazard. The time was about midnight and I brought some hot coffee up to the watchman to help keep him awake. The signalman on duty that night was a smart and funny inner city African American that I had befriended early in my tour on board the Reclaimer.

The signalman and I sipped coffee and joked about girls we were seeing in Honolulu for a while until his face lost all expression and he looked past me. The signalman was just staring towards the front of the ship and off the bow. I turned to see what he was concerned about and I could not believe my eyes. In the dark of night, with no clouds, the huge moon shining in the sky had created a strange phenomenon. A sort of rainbow effect only in a shimmering white arc, not in the myriad of colors usually seen. I had never heard or seen such a beautiful thing before, the glowing arc from the moon's light above the ocean was amazing.

The signalman and I looked at the shimmering arc for a long time and then back at each other. The Reclaimer was heading for the arc of light as the ship would pass right underneath it. The arc grew closer and larger and it took on a three dimensional look.

I wondered if either of us should notify someone. For what? I thought. This beautiful arc of night light was not a threat to the Reclaimer. The ship was not going to collide with. This light was something else. Less dangerous yet more profound than anything else I had experienced in nature on the ocean. The signalman and I just stood there and stared at it.

The Reclaimer continued forward at its usual pace of around 8 knots. I wondered if anyone else was seeing this. The two or three sailors below us on the bridge were probably going over navigation charts and checking out satellite locations. The rest of the ship's crew was either asleep or on watch in the engine rooms. Most likely it was just the two of us up on the top deck.

When the Reclaimer arrived at the arc itself I figured it would dissipate just as a rainbow does when a person gets near it. The moon's glowing arc did not dissipate. The bright white arc, about as half as bright as the moon in the sky itself, went right over the Reclaimer. The ship had gone under and through the arc like crossing under a bridge. As the Reclaimer moved on the arc stayed in its original place and fell away behind the Reclaimer's path. The signalman and I turned to watch the arc go over us and beyond.

My mouth was wide open and I turned to look at my friend. Watching the gentle arc of light pass over me was a bizarre experience. After a while the arc was not visible anymore. With out saying anything about what I had seen I gathered up my music and books and went below. The signalman and I never spoke about the experience again, for some strange reason. The signalman, my friend, committed suicide about a year later on board the ship over circumstances that are personal to him and his family so I will not go into them in this book out of respect.

When I told this story to ship mates from the Reclaimer they figures I was just tired or I was dreaming. Either way it was an interesting experience and I am glad to have had it with my friend before he took his life. He was a good person and that is all I can say.

When the Reclaimer arrived in Panama, at the small naval base that protected the Western mouth of the canal, I saw the submarine waiting to be towed. The decommissioned nuclear sub looked like a new ship, for all I knew about submarines. The sub was modern looking, smooth, black and was marked with the usual water line numbers that were painted on a vessel that was stricken and under tow. The technology inside the submarine may have been outdated, but it looked ready to go on the outside.

The vessel that towed the submarine through the Panama canal was quite a sight. The ship was one of the oldest vessels in the United States Navy. An AT ship or Auxiliary Tow vessel. The AT still had the round shaped bridge tower from the world war two navy days and looked straight out of an old war movie. What a sight. The AT was three quarters the size of the Reclaimer and had a crew compliment of about sixty men. What a miserable duty that must have been!

In opposition to my thoughts, the AT's crew were in amazingly high moral and walked across the pier to help the Reclaimer tie up. Once the lines were secure our two ships sat on opposite sides from each other across the pier. Two old ships still chugging along in this modern navy. The sailors from the AT exchanged ball caps and patches with the Reclaimer's crew , an old custom in the navy when ship's crews met. Later the two crews agreed to barbeque and drink some beers together before they took off for their destinations.

The first day in Panama the Reclaimer's crew made sure the submarine was ready for the trip up the coast line to Seattle. The travel would be a long way and master diver Starkey wanted the sub secured tight.

Master diver Starkey had worked on salvage vessels for so long that he knew all the tricks. Starkey had the Reclaimer's divers run lines to the submarine and back and used it as a pull line to yank the Reclaimer's huge steel tow cable over to the sub. The tow cable was thousands of pounds of braided/spun steel wire about three inches thick and took a group of divers to heave from one side of the Reclaimer's fantail to the other.

Just a note here. Salvage ships do not use brute force to do heavy jobs. Vessels like the Reclaimer use raw torque to yank a stranded ship off of a coral bed and for long, heavy tows the ship used science. Physics to be exact. When the Reclaimer was designed it was to be capable of moving and manipulating much larger ships around than itself. Aircraft carriers and the like. This required a practical use of physics to be possible.

The way the Reclaimer towed a ship across the ocean was by using the weight of the steel tow cable itself.

The Reclaimer would give a constant pull on the cable and maintain a steady course and speed. The heavy braided steel tow cable would droop down low in the ocean and then pull tight. When the tow cable lost slack it would pull on the ship the Reclaimer was towing. The real trick was that the tow cable would never go completely taught unless a massive pull was taken on it. The inertia built up in the weight of the tow cable "inch wormed" the vessel behind the Reclaimer along. That was the trick. The tow line would go slack again and you would just keep pulling along. If you could speed it up it would look like an upside down inchworm.

Starkey had the Reclaimer's divers rig the tow cable to the sub using huge "U" shaped steel bits that weighed at least a hundred pounds. The master diver also had back up systems in place in case the submarine's load became too much for the Reclaimer's tow machine to handle and the sub had to be disconnected. For that purpose Starkey rigged a one arm folding steel device to the tow chain called a Pelican Link (after the shape that looked like the jaws of a pelican). If there was a storm during the tow or if the submarine started to take on water faster than the Reclaimer's dive team could remove it, the tow cable would be disconnected through the pelican link; the jaws would open and the submarine would be free. This was a back up plan for an emergency only and would require significant effort on the dive team to perform and then somehow recover the submarine after. In high seas, someone would most likely get thrown from the ship doing this.

The Reclaimer's divers laid out back up chains, more "U" shaped bits and a other equipment. If our team needed a piece of equipment fast, Starkey did not want us running around the ship looking for stuff. The master diver wanted everything on the fantail, tied to the bulkheads and ready to go.

The Reclaimer needed a handful of repairs and a good amount of gray paint after the long, three week, crossing from Honolulu to Panama. The crew spent the rest of the day and well into the night painting and fixing the Recalimer for the upcoming tow.

That night the Reclaimer's crew drank and ate with the AT crew as well as the Panama base sailors. The majority of sailors stationed in Panama were small boat operators working with navy Seals to protect the Panama Canal. Much of the world's economy rested on the shipping that flowed through the canal and the United States took it's security very seriously.

Now that the Reclaimer was touched up and ready for the tow up the coast, the crew was given an orientation on the Panama Canal area. The crew would be given a day or two to visit Panama City and surrounding tourist sites. That sounded humorous considering that the United States just blew the main city to pieces just weeks before the Reclaimer arrived. Now sailors were supposed to go out and sight see? A bunch of half lit American servicemen? Sounded good to me. After three weeks on that tin can crossing the Pacific the crew was ready to see some land. I think if the Reclaimer had pulled into North Korea for refueling the crew would have requested shore leave.

The divers decided to get a group together and travel to the Panama canal locks themselves. The Canal locks were considered the main tourist destination in the Panama City area so the dive locker team figured they would be a good place to start. The orientation by the Panama naval base representatives that morning said that the route between the base and the locks was the safest way to choose. The Panama base sailors also said that the crew was in danger of getting killed for our clothing and money just about anywhere we go, so no route could really be called "safe". That was nice.

The divers from the various Reclaimer departments got together and set off for the Panama base front gates to get a cab or whatever sort of transportation was available. The Panama naval base was locked down with soldiers and heavy equipment to prevent attacks from Noriega loyalists still lurking in the jungle around the installation. At the front gates the divers were told a taxi would be coming by every few minutes to get sailors and take them into town.

Moments later a red four door Honda with mismatch wheels and rust destroyed paint came careening around the corner and towards the gate. The other divers and I figured it was some sort of an attack so we stayed behind the guard shack to give the soldiers room for the upcoming firefight. The Panama naval base guards just stood there and smoked cigarettes.

The red, poor excuse for a car came to a halt in front of the base gate with a screech of worn brakes. The sound of just metal on metal. A local man wearing a white short sleeved shirt and stained pants came out with his hands waving and an smile on his face. The driver did not speak enough English to do any good so the divers tried to point at areas on our Panama map. After a while the base guards told us the driver was one of the local taxi owners and helped us communicate for a ride.

I explained that our group wanted to go into town and see the locks. Well, that was two different things. The "town" part the driver understood well, he must have been paid by a local bar owner on the side for bringing sailors into town to spend money. Instead of the Panama Canal locks our group was driven, packed like sardines in that damn car, into Panama City,

Panama. The red vehicle came to a screeching halt just missing a cement wall and the divers were dropped off. The cab was not expensive and after his payment the driver left the area as fast as he had arrived.

Looking around e I could see why the driver was in such a hurry. The part of town our group was in was in total ruins. This section of Panama City looked as if it had always been the "seedy" area, but now, after the American attack, this area was even worse with bullet holes and bomb damage to the surrounding buildings.

Our group stood out bad. Our skin was bright white as most of the divers worked inside the ship while underway and had no tan. Each of us wore bright colored, flowered aloha shirts (the traditional civilian wear of divers in the Navy). I surveyed the damage done to the homes and businesses and decided to have our group stay together.

Moving towards the rubble I noticed that businesses had not shut down after the attacks on the city. Instead the shops were still open after the damage. Bars, liquor stores, restaurants, small food stores all were operating with generators and electric fans blowing inside. In front of each store was a man with a 12 gauge shotgun for protection from looters.

I thought our group would be targeted by these locals for elimination. We were not. The Panamanians smiled at our group and those who could speak English asked if we were looking for somewhere in particular. It would seem that the majority of the local population looked at Americans as liberators from Noriega. Our group was not treated bad or threatened by anyone. It was a pleasant surprise.

One of the store owners directed me to the center of town. What a change. After a few miles of walking our group of aloha shirt wearing freaks came to the financial district of Panama City. Sky scrapers and businesses were open and the streets were clean. Traffic lights worked and sports cars were driving to various destinations. It seemed like another world from the one our group had just come out of.

High end clothing stores and American restaurants were everywhere. I actually had lunch at a Pizza Hut! I could not believe it. In that city, just after the attack, Pizza hut was ready to go. The local pizza was not the same, though, as Panamanians used goat's milk cheese on the pizza instead of cow's milk cheese. This was not a big problem for a bunch of guys who had been eating mystery food from a silver can for three weeks. The pizza tasted just fine.

The beer in Panama comes in small cans. The taste was fine if they were at least cold. After our meal the divers caught another cab from Panama City to the actual Panama canal locks.

The locks were kept very clean with fresh paint used everywhere. It was a tourist attraction and there were visiting families from all over the world taking pictures. The tourists spoke several languages like German or Italian.

My map showed tourist destinations such as pirate castles along the coast. Our group hired some cabs and we left the canal for the castles. Along the way the local children waited at stop lights and would try to sell vehicle passengers bread and beer on the street. Right into the car windows. The children were wearing small beer can tabs, cut sharp like little knives, on their fingertips. At first I thought it was to go after tourist's for their money, but they never did. When I asked the taxi driver why they all wore the little blades on their fingers he gestured as if to reach out and grab some one and hold them. Apparently kidnapping was big in Panama and the kids wore the beer caps to cut someone who would try to grab them and drag them into the car. In a third world country it was no secret that kids were often kidnapped and killed for kidneys and other valuable organs.

The pirate castles of Panama are a hidden wonder. If only it was safer to travel in this country, I am sure thousands would love to see the beautiful coast and historical sites along the way. The divers walked among the huge ruins of the castles and took pictures together.

Panama was a poor and divided nation. The beautiful ruins of ancient pirate castles were a sight I wish all could see. In Panama, people were just trying to survive and there was little government stability. The sight of poor children trying to sell food by the roads, knowing that they were targets for kidnapping, was hard for me to take at about twenty years old. It made me respect what I had as an American. I understood what it was I cherished about my country and wanted to protect.

After a few hours of wandering around the ruins, I headed back for the waiting cabs and our group headed back for the naval base.

Nightlife in Panama was not safe for Americans as opportunist muggers and thieves worked the local bars and nightclubs. For that reason the Air Force base, next to the Naval base, decided to use one of its older buildings and convert it into a huge entertainment center. The air force enlisted club had pool tables, several different bars and forms of music playing inside, all in different rooms. The sailors and airmen now had a place to go hang out that was relatively safe.

Even local Panamanian girls could go to the place, but they had to undergo security checks before entering the base. Many of the young Panamanian women saw the air base as a way to find American husbands and hundreds would flood the enlisted club each weekend.

Hearing this the Reclaimer sailors decided to check out the establishment. The divers caught a transport together and piled into the bars. By the time the Reclaimer sailors arrived at the air base club, late, the place was full of sailors, soldiers and airmen. The enlisted club was officially a mad house.

Lights, liquor and music playing loud. Each bar inside the building was more crazy than the last. The Panamanian girls are beautiful with dark skin and brown eyes . I imagined this was a good place to visit, but, a dangerous place to get stationed. The Reclaimer's divers drank and danced until about two a.m. when a fight broke out between, well, who knows and base security started to close the place up.

The streets outside of the club were filled with servicemen laughing, arguing, fighting and drinking. I soon noticed that it was well past the last shuttle time and I was miles from the naval base. One of the dive officers who was with our group reminded me that the captain wanted everyone checked in by three a.m. It was about two thirty and our group was not even on the same base.

Our group of divers started to run. The air force guards at the front of the base directed our group down a long and unlit road to find the naval installation. The guards told us it was about an hour walk. The half-drunk rabble and I took off down the road at full speed. The running and high humidity made me sick as I tore along the dark path.

By three a.m. the team was at the naval base gates and panting for air. I helped carry a few guys who were too sick to continue to the ship and stumbled on board. Thank god the captain and XO were asleep. Several members of the crew were talking in the mess decks and on the fantail about the night. I moved a few guys down the ship's ladders and into their bunks. I laughed with the rest of the divers in the ship's dive locker below decks about the night and fell asleep.

The next morning the Reclaimer was underway and heading north for the United States west coast.

The Reclaimer pulled into San Diego, California as our tow mission's next port. San Diego was a port much loved by sailors for its fun nightlife and college town environment. The Reclaimer tied up next to several larger warships, and attracted the usual questions from the sailors aboard them such as "What kind of ship is that?" and "are they active navy or , like, reservists." When the Reclaimer pulled into port, looking like a floating museum, it stood out from the high technology cruisers and destroyers moored within the harbor.

Our captain gave the Reclaimer's crew the night off to hit the town and let off some steam. A group of divers from the dive locker got together with some of the crew to hit the enlisted club that was built just outside the naval base grounds. Morgan, a good friend of mine and one of the Reclaimer's cooks, went with our group.

Morgan was a tough Louisiana Frenchmen from New Orleans. Like my other friends on board the Recalimer, Mcnamara, Gordon, Baxter and the rest, we were from very different backgrounds. On the Reclaimer each of our crew had to deal with the hardship of junk-boat life and backgrounds were arbitrary to camaraderie.

The enlisted club at San Diego was a riot. The club had a full sized wrestling ring built into the center of the establishment. The ring doubled as a dance floor when the music was playing and a full scale brawl when the night got late and the sailors got looped. Sailors would challenge each other in the ring for full scale wrestling matches, dressed in civilian clothes, and wagers were placed between various ship's top brawlers.

San Diego had always been a college town, but there were not as many clubs and established bars back in early 1990's when the Reclaimer pulled in. The beach clubs in San Diego were always packed so sailors were forced to find smaller, out of the way spots. The Reclaimer divers had heard about the bar featured in the movie Top Gun with the piano. This tiny, dimly lit liquor joint was practically empty and our group had a good time singing and drinking until late while some unknown drunk played the piano.

After the piano bar our group wandered into a coffee shop down the street and I had a few shots of espresso to sober up. The divers and I walked in and took a few tables near the window, unfortunately the seats we chose were next to a group of would-be poets arguing about rhymes and ideas. One of the divers seated next to the Kerouac-wanna-bes noticed a thesaurus in their stack of books and started to yell out, calling them frauds.

What a mess, both tables were standing, screaming and ready to throw fists. A few divers and myself were on the other side of the coffee shop talking with some cute college girls. (I had been in Hawaii for some time by now and I was mesmerized by the tall blonde girls of San Diego, California.) I looked over to the divers and writers just as they started to throw each other around the establishment. Everything fell apart and we were tossed out, of a coffee shop mind you, and our two groups separated outside.

91

The divers stumbled down the road and broke up to go our separate ways. Some guys took cabs back to base while others were committed to finding an open bar. My Cajun friend and I walked along the train tracks that led through the industrial district of San Diego and towards base.

When a train came slowly rumbling by, blaring its horn at Morgan and I to get the hell out of the way, the two of us grabbed the ladders on a box car and rode the train for several miles back to base. I waved at the cars stopped along the way at railroad stop lights. After a half hour or so I could see the naval base and jumped off.

The next day the Reclaimer was reloaded with food and supplies and it headed up the coast line towards the north western United States. The divers of the Reclaimer had a way of leaving a lasting impression on the cities we pulled into.

One of the most beautiful ports any sailor could pull into was the Seattle, Washington naval installation, actually at Bremerton, Washington, and the surrounding port region. There were several smaller ports that a ship could tie up at once it entered the long and beautiful channel that weaves its way into Seattle harbor. As I stated earlier in this book, the submarine base located there was one of the nicest bases in the U.S. navy.

Seattle was also the home of one of the navy's largest inactive ships yard. As the Reclaimer pulled through this yard I stood on the fantail of the ship with a cup of coffee and looked at the rows of world war two naval vessels resting in the "inac-ship" yard. Huge aircraft carriers and mighty cruisers from the bygone era now awaited the scrap yard. The Reclaimer was older than many of these ships which gave me a noble feeling as our vessel, still active and underway, slowly cruised by.

The waterway that took the Reclaimer into Seattle was wide enough for our ship to pass through without trouble, but it could become dangerous fast with the submarine in tow behind us. The Reclaimer's turns had to be timed just right so as not to collide the load with either side of the water way. Both sides of the winding passage were lined with multi-million dollar homes, so our captain did not want to take out someone's boat house with a derelict nuclear submarine under tow. That would have been quite a sight to watch from a homeowner's back porch over morning coffee.

Another danger was the stress that sharp turns put on the Reclaimer's tow cable. The tow machine itself could only hold so much weight. If the weight exceeded the tow machine's maximum range there was the possibility that the tow machine would rip from the Reclaimer's fantail. The tow cable would not break, it was several inches thick of spun-woven steel. The tow cable was made of the kind of steel wire that held up bridges. The weak point was a series of metal bolts that held the tow machine to the Reclaimer's deck. It was those bolts that would break first. Not good. Let me just say that.

As the Reclaimer rounded each turn through the water way, heading into Seattle Harbor, master diver Starkey had a full damage control team waiting just inside the skin of the ship to deal with the after effects of an over-stress pull on the tow line.   Starkey had seen salvage vessels and ship's under tow get damaged from various issues before in his career, but he did not talk about it. The fact that the master diver had a crew set up to deal with everything from fires to a tear in the Reclaimer's hull explained that Starkey knew the risks involved that day.

There I was, geared up in protective helmets, gloves, face masks and coveralls. Another diver, Baxter, was geared up with me and we waited with a sledge hammer and wire cutters next to the tow cable. Too damn close to the tow cable. Our job was to cut the seizing wire and throw open the steel jaws of the "pelican link" if the stress on the tow cable became so bad that the tow machine was in danger of ripping loose.

A small gauge on the Reclaimer's tow machine read how high a pull the tow cable had on it at any given time. While underway, the Reclaimer would take ocean waves and rolling seas causing the gauge to read moderate and even heavy pulls on the steel cable that connected the submarine to our vessel. Now, as the Reclaimer passed through this twisting waterway, each turn took the gauge beyond the maximum range of the tow machine's mounting bolts.

Technically the Reclaimer should have ripped open several times sending the submarine drifting until the steel chain-links that master diver Starkey had affixed to the tow cable could take the strain. The Reclaimer did not break even under the hard strains. That damn old salvage boat surprised the crew time and time again.

With each turn the Reclaimer escaped without damage to either vessel. Baxter and I stood at the ready with our tools as we came into the final turn. Master diver Starkey was calling out the speed and direction orders for the Reclaimer's bridge. An officer on the level above the fantail was leaning over and listening to changes yelled out by Starkey and relaying them to the bridge crew.

Well into one turn the cable came taught and the stress levels on the tow machine began to peg all the way beyond maximum again. The watchman at the tow machine called out to master diver Starkey with the strain gauge readings, but Starkey could already tell the Reclaimer was taking too much. The master diver ordered Baxter and I to walk up to the pelican link and stand by. Shuffling up to the link, Baxter and I stayed very close with our boots almost touching. The procedure of cutting the wire and throwing the jaws had to be done as a team and fast.

One of the Bremerton naval base tug boats was heading toward the Reclaimer in this distance to assist with the tow as the Reclaimer was rounding into the harbor itself. All that was left was to make this last turn, and the Reclaimer would release the submarine to the harbor tug. With all the stress on the tow cable Starkey could see the Reclaimer would not take anymore. There was no more time.

The Reclaimer made several noises like thick metal bending. The command was given, master diver Starkey yelled to Baxter and I to through the pelican jaws and get the hell out of the way. The back up plan to the tow machine had to be set in motion.

The idea went like this, if the pelican jaws were thrown open, the weight would come off of the tow machine and onto the thick, steel chain links. The chain was secured hard to the ships fantail and would not break. If the submarine decided to sink with the chain links attached to the tow line, the Reclaimer was going down with it. That was why it was called a "back up plan."

Baxter and I made the last two steps up to the pelican link and leaned forward. The link had a pin to keep the jaws shut and a light wire called seizing-wire was used to keep the pin in place. Just as Baxter went to cut the seizing wire, one of the steel salvage links attached to the tow cable and Pelican link bent from straight to the shape of the letter "V" from the heavy strain. The steel pin, which was about three inches thick, had decades of paint coatings on it. The layers of dried paint exploded and struck Baxter and I like shrapnel from a land mine. We both fell backwards from the force and scrambled to get away from the link.

Several officers watching from the level above the fantail began to yell out orders to clear the area. Officers shouted out for the divers working the tow line to get inside the skin of the ship so as not to be knocked into the water when the tow machine ripped from it's support bolts.

The sound of bending metal continued and the Pelican link was still in place. Baxter and I were crawling on our bellies to get away from the bending link, we knew it would not save us as the tow machine would drive right into the two of us on the fantail when it tore loose.

The next few seconds played out like slow motion for me. I watched as master diver Starkey walked out onto the fantail directly into the path of the tow machine and stood right over the pelican link. Starkey picked up the sledge hammer that I had dropped and swung it at the jaws of the link. With a loud clang and a few sparks the jaws of the pelican link flung open and the tow cable jerked from the machine to the ship's chain links secured to the fantail. Pieces of broken steel links bounced around the deck.

The tow machine stopped making the high stress noises. Starkey threw down the sledge hammer and walked over to where Baxter and I were lying flat on the fantail deck. He looked down at us and muttered some obscenities. Just then I saw that Starkey had never even dropped the lit cigarette in his other hand. That was one hard core son of a bitch.

The dive team stayed clear of the tow line as it swung from one end of the Reclaimer's fan tail to the other. The naval base tug was acting fast to secure itself to the submarine and share the load with our vessel. The timing could not have been any closer. With the submarine under the tug's control I worked with Baxter to disengage the Reclaimer's heavy steel chain from the tow line and the submarine was gone. The tug crew would take the sub to it's final resting place in the inactive ship yard. Hey, The Reclaimer had got the damn thing to Seattle in one piece, we were lucky to get that.

Alive and still floating, the Reclaimer pulled into Bremerton, Washington just across the bay from Seattle. The divers broke down the tow gear and cleared the damaged steel links. The Reclaimer crew rolled out fire hoses to give the ship a fresh water wash down. The Recliamer has tied up next to a Nimitz class aircraft carrier at the Bremerton naval yards. We looked like a row boat next to that thing. Several sailors were leaning over the rails of the carrier and watching our boat pull in. Their tiny heads and blue ball caps were visible from the carrier decks many stories above our ship.

It was a relief to wash down and clean up the ship after the tow. There were water fights and crew members threw sponges at each other. The Reclaimer was going home in a few days, back to Hawaii. First, a good stay in Seattle.

The naval base in Bremerton is huge and houses thousands of shore based sailors. In order to get to the city of Seattle from Bremerton a sailor walked from base to a ferry landing. These huge ferries took vehicles and pedestrians across the harbor in long slow crossings. The ferries were only available until around midnight, which meant once the Reclaimer guys crossed over to Seattle, they needed to stay there until five in the morning, when the first ferries headed out for Bremerton to pick up morning commuters.

The divers and I checked out with Starkey and headed for the ferry landing. We made a stop at a small store on base to pick up several brown paper bags full of hard liquor. It was going to be a long ride across the water to Seattle and I figured carrying cases of beer on board would attract too much attention. The Reclaimer's dive team and I paid our fares and walked up to the main pedestrian traffic deck on the ferry.

The Seattle ferry left around six p.m. which meant it was full of Bremerton sailors. It was Friday, the end of the work week and everyone was ready to relax. Our group talked and passed around the bottles of rum and Kentucky whiskey to fight off the cold.

The Reclaimer arrived in Seattle during the cold part of the year and the wind chill made the temperature worse. I had noticed the temperature dropping during the trip up the coastline from San Diego. The Reclaimer had begun the trip from the warm climates of Hawaii and Panama. Even Sand Diego was not very cold regardless of the season. Seattle was not a frozen land like the Midwest I grew up in, but it fell to near zero at night.

The ferry landing at Seattle emptied directly onto the lower boardwalk area of the city. Seattle was a very interesting town. It was built on the sloping hills around the harbor. The hills were steep which meant streets had to be built up from the water and steep grade with huge wood and steel girders. The city of Seattle itself rested on a superstructure designed by early architects. Underneath the streets of Seattle there were pockets of "old Seattle" that still remained. The buildings that were built directly onto the hill sides were covered and lost under the massive superstructure as it was built. Some of this historical district could be visited as it was restored and turned into a museum.

The ferry landing was on the lower waterline section of Seattle. I stepped off the ferry into a dark and deserted part of town. Ferry travelers walked over to the parking lots to pick up their cars and go home. I had about some good night life in Seattle from the local sailors and headed for a district known as Pioneer Square.

Most of the navy crowd went into a bar that played rock and roll music live and loud. The music spilled out into the street and park fronting the establishment. This park and surrounding bars was Pioneer Square. The area was well designed as several taverns, live music joints and a pizza shop faced the central square shaped park where a bar-hopper could relax in between forays. For the divers of the Reclaimer the park benches were stopping points to regroup between getting thrown out of various night spots.

I proceeded to try several bars as our team made our way around the square. Navy divers traditionally tried to steer clear of any bar that had a reputation for too many military patrons. Divers were often dressed different from other sailors and our hair tended to be too long to be confused for military. For that reason divers patronized less crowded bars and restaurants that remained off the beaten path.

We played pool and drank until around one a.m. After that I stumbled into the square and found an all night pizza parlor shining like a bright red and yellow lit church in the cold Seattle night. The heat from the ovens and the smell of fresh pizza attracted dozens of Seattle party goers and turned out to be a great place to meet girls. Stuck in line for pizza I gabbed with chicks and invited them to the next establishment. Which they led me to, of course, as I was the stranger in a strange land.

The late hours of the Seattle night were spent at what would become my favorite book store in the world, the Elliot Bay Book Factory. Open until around two in the morning, I sat and read books, drank coffee and talked to cute Seattle ladies until the place closed.

It was early in the morning, about three a.m. and I met up with the other divers near the ferry landing. There were no scheduled ferries for hours so we stood by the gates to the landing and talked for a while. Over the conversation I heard a saxophone playing blues music from somewhere in the dark night. The dive team wandered towards the sound and came upon a small, all African American, blues bar down on the water line of the city, about a quarter mile from the ferry landing.

The bar was about half full and the crowd watched us as our all-white group piled in. We were obviously intoxicated, but we did not plan to drive anywhere so the bartender set us up with several pitchers of some beer from Alaska that was on sale. The patrons inside whispered about our odd-ball group and looked confused as to why we were there. Hey, it was open and still serving. Any further questions?

I knew several of the tunes playing and I have to say it was some of the best jazz and blues I had ever heard. Two loud sax players, one soprano and the other bass, worked off of each other as a great back up band woke up the house with tune after tune.

The Reclaimer divers drank and chilled out until the place closed and we were, once again, on the street. Cold and without shelter we made our way back to the landing and hoped for the first ferry to arrive. No luck. It was still an hour until the first ferry and the wind was biting cold.

Our group of about eight crawled under the heavy plastic matting that fronted the ferry landing. We used this filthy mat as a blanket for a good hour of sleep as we waited. The ground was concrete and frozen which leeched the body heat right out of me. By the time the ferry came along, I was stiff with cold and shuffled my way to the upper deck to pass out on a ferry bench.

Seattle gave the Reclaimer crew several great nights of fun. The divers made the late night book store and blues bar the required ending to each night for our group. Word to the wise, do not drink heavy and then ride to the top of the Seattle space needle. Not the best experience.

During our stop in Seattle the divers were assigned to perform an after action hull inspection on the Reclaimer. Such a long tow could damage an old vessel and the captain wanted to make a last inspection before The Reclaimer left port for Honolulu. Master Diver Starkey had the ship's divers set up dive station on the fantail.

The chosen dive rig was the heavy navy wet suits we were issued and the Mark 12 hard hat dive rig to give the divers both head protection when working under the steel hull and to get some valuable hard hat diving station experience. The Reclaimer dive team went to work for several hours cruising the hull of the Reclaimer with flashlights.

The water in Seattle is very cold. I wore my heavy wet suit that was given to me upon arrival at the Reclaimer. The suit helped, but the cold seeped right through and eventually froze my extremities. I kept my arms and legs moving to push hot blood through them and prevent numbness.

I was surprised to find the quality of the water in the Bremerton naval yards to be quite good. It was dark and I only had a few feet of vision, but it was clean harbor water and not contaminated with oil spills and sludge. Some naval bases have poor water conditions and diving in them can be miserable.

During my inspection dive I wore the Mark 12 helmet with a harness that held it down onto my shoulders. The helmet was bright yellow and bobbed around from the force of air being pumped down to me from the dive station above. The comms were, as usual, not working so my dive buddy and I gave pull signals to the dive supervisor when needed. The supervisor gave me the signal for a return to the surface and my buddy and I slowly rose up from under the hull.

Master Diver Starkey pointed down to me in the water and talked to the supervisor running the dive station. The supervisor was one of our first class divers. The sup' leaned over the ship's fantail and explained that a bag of tools had been lost near the area of the dive station by one of the Reclaimer's engineers working on the fantail in the last couple of days. The supervisor wanted me to go down and find it. Apparently, it was a large canvas bag that had enough tools inside to warrant a bottom drop.

I looked over to my dive "buddy" and signaled I was going down. We both signaled the dive supervisor and slipped beneath the water. We were tied together with a line about six feet in length to prevent one of us from getting too far from the other in the low, hell, negative visibility. I checked my depth several times and used my flashlight to signal the other diver as we went lower.

Bremerton harbor was not deep, but it had the ability to handle major ships like aircraft carriers so the water was a good 100 feet down before I hit mud. I placed my helmet mask right up to the other diver's and signaled him that I was going to bend down and look for the bag.

I had to move slow so as not to stir up the bottom sediment and loose whatever miserable visibility I had with my flash light. As I stepped through the mud I gave the line between my buddy diver and I a tug to signal my position. It was some time in that black and cold harbor before I found the bag. I felt it with my foot and reached down to pick it up.

I was sure that my dive partner was just as frozen by now as I was so I turned around to give the line a good yank and take us back to the surface. Before I could grab the line my buddy bumped into me hard enough to knock me off my feet and I went deep into the mud, on my back. The tool bag made it worse as I sunk even further into the muck. I was too cold to worry about the mud and I figured we would clean it off on deck with the water hoses. I lifted myself back to a seated position and reached in front of me to find my buddy.

I felt him directly in front of me with my right hand. I reached back for the flashlight, that was tied to my waist belt with a small line, and brought the light beam forward. I leaned forward so as to see in the one foot of visibility the small flashlight gave me. I looked forward through the Mark 12 helmet front glass plate and found myself looking into a large eyeball about the size of a dinner plate. I did not care what it was or what it was intending to do, I scrambled out of the mud and yanked on the buddy line as I began to kick my fins hard for the surface. I was breathing hard and I did not even feel the extra weight of the canvas bag full of tools.

I pulled the line that connected my buddy to me until I had his arm and we broke the water surface together. He looked at me as if to ask what the hell was going on. We had some help climbing back aboard and gave the supervisor our times and depths. The dive station workers hosed us down for a while and Starkey called the morning quits for lunch.

I was finished with the hull inspection and I had found the stinking bag of junk. I made my way to the hot showers and mess decks to thaw out. I will never forget that dive in Bremerton, the harbor is full of sea life there.

Some a little stranger than others. I still love to tell that story when asked about my navy diving years.

The submarine tow mission was one of the USS Reclaimer's final major missions in the vessel's six decades of active service. It will be remembered by me and many others as a wild time and a great trip.

Chapter 6.
First you sink 'em then you raise 'em.

Every two years the navy challenged the dive communities in Hawaii to a duel. Each would have to demonstrate the skills and capabilities required of them in a time of war. For the EOD and SEAL divers it was to insert into an enemy harbor and sabotage the fleet stationed there. For the Salvage Diving, or deep sea, community it was to repair major damages to ships and even raise those that had been sunk.

The result of these peace time tests was a biennial contest between the various teams in Pearl Harbor. The EOD and SEAL divers would sink a mothballed ship in the harbor and the deep sea group would repair and raise it. It was a good test of our abilities. It allowed us to work out problems and find new ideas that would save time in a war zone.

The chosen prey of the SEAL teams was an oil transport that had been used by the navy around the time of Vietnam. The transport was about as long as the Reclaimer, but much lighter as most of the ship was open spaces to carry fuel and oil inside. The transport was designed with crew berthing at one end and a raised bridge. It had a long catwalk that connected the forward and aft superstructures and allowed the crew to move easier than along the cluttered main deck. Large steel lids capped off the various inner spaces for liquid storage. It made a good and realistic target for the commandos.

The oil transport was towed to a distant end of Pear Harbor for the demolition phase of the operation. This area would prevent the explosives used from damaging new and active warships that were tied up on the East side of the harbor. It was rather close to a park used by civilians for weekend picnics along Pearl Harbor which gave us an audience each day we worked at raising the transport. Sometimes the afternoon lunch crowds would drive down to the park to see our dive team working. It may have been confusing to onlookers and I am sure some of them thought a ship had actually sunk in the harbor by accident.

The Reclaimer got underway early in the morning. The night before had been the SEAL team phase of the test. The oil transport had been sunk with several small satchel charges no doubt brought in from the mouth of the harbor by a SEAL team using SCUBA rebreathers. Rebreathers were basic SCUBA systems with a separate attachment that prevented the bubbles from rising up after each exhale. Bubbles could give away the teams position and had to be prevented for commando style operations. The re-breathers sent the exhaled air into a "scrubber" that removed as much of the CO_2 as it could and reused the left over O_2 again.

The Reclaimer was positioned close to the transport and dropped anchor. As the Reclaimer had a relatively flat or at least a "whale" shaped bottom, we could get quite close and not fear getting stuck in the mud ourselves. Forward of the Recalimer was the aft end, fantail, of the oil transport. The transport's catwalk went down and into the water to a sunken bow and forecastle. Seeing the transport half sunk made me think how it must have been for salvage ships, maybe even the Reclaimer, to raise vessels in the Pacific theater of WWII. The shallow water battles that were fought near Pacific islands often made it possible to raise and recover lost ships.

Master Diver Starkey was more concerned about the transport's list to starboard. He realized that if the vessel were to slide over further it could crush and kill divers attempting to patch holes blown in the starboard side hull. For that reason Starkey decided the list had to be corrected first and then the repairs.

The two fifty foot workboats that the Reclaimer carried were lowered and rigged as temporary dive stations. Each workboat would carry steel plates and welding equipment to begin locating and repairing damage. The dive team loaded up the boats with dive gear and damage control supplies.

The two work boats gave the Reclaimer the ability to divide into three platforms in order to accomplish tasks. Each fifty foot boat was a flat bottom, steel landing craft complete with the lowering forward door/ramp. Divers used the boats for everything they could think of from diving platforms to hauling heavy gear around a harbor. The work boats acted as tugs when the Reclaimer was towing ships, they carried men and supplies, they did the dirty work in the dirty jobs.

Our inspection dives were first directed to the interiors of the ship. Starkey was concerned about the starboard list and he had the first few dive groups search for hull damage that had caused the lean to one side. Detonating the starboard charges first and then the rest would have sunk the ship with a starboard list. It could also have been a boulder in the mud that the transport was resting on. The divers would enter the transport using the large steel lids that led into each of the oil storage spaces below.

The Reclaimer's dive teams used SCUBA and the newer Superlight 17 hard hat rigs to get into and around the transport. The navy likes to see hard hat diving in cases when you had to enter a sunken vessel. The Reclaimer held our Superlight 17 dive platform and air supplies for hard hat diving. The SCUBA stations were set up on the fifty foot work boats. Only SCUBA could go beyond the ship itself. These were just the kind of problems that divers were supposed to come across and overcome.

The navy does have portable dive systems that can be carried anywhere, including on a fifty foot landing craft. The "fly away" systems, as they were called, were easy enough to request in the case of real emergency. The idea of this test was to not have all the resources a master diver could dream for. Instead Starkey had to adapt to the limited capabilities of the Reclaimer just as if our ship were thousands of miles from an American naval base.

Master Diver Starkey decided to use a steel and rubber temporary patch system to move faster with the recovery operation. One the transport was made level, divers in Superlight 17 helmets could weld steel plates over holes in the side for a more permanent fix. Hull technicians from the Reclaimer could re-weld the damage later when the ship was up and yanked from the mud.

The patches were square or round plates of steel with matching sheets of thick rubber attached. A hole was drilled through each and a long steel bolt was fed through the hole. These patches would be placed up to the holes in the transport's hull after divers had spent hours pounding at the holes with sledge hammers to make them as flat as possible. On the outside of the patches would go steel bars that, when nuts on both ends were tightened, would hold the patches onto the hull and seal the holes.

Divers in Superlight 17 hard hat rigs could stay inside the ship and affix the steel bars through the hull. The nuts on the inside could be tightened and after a few hours yellow gear pumps from the Reclaimer would be used to pump the space dry. Well, it may still leak through the patch, but the idea was to have the salvage pumps work faster than the leaks.

Starkey sat back and discussed the various patches with dive teams as welders cut out the needed plates. The dive team had turned the transport into a work platform on one end and the fifty foot boats could now shuttle supplies and food between the ship and our divers. By the end of the day Starkey had the holes in at least two spaces hammered flat and both were patched for water removal.

Using the Superlight 17 dive rigs, divers were able to weld temporary patches in damages spaces that could not take a rubber patch effectively. It was always good training and experience to perform underwater welding work. The Reclaimer's divers included some damn good welders that provided the second class divers on board, like me, with the opportunity to watch and assist them in the patch process.

The next step was to set up lights for night work and run a generator. The work boats brought several yellow gear water pumps to the transport which had to be man handled by our team into place and tied down to keep them from sliding into the water due to the list. The pumps were very heavy, they were designed to be lifted and placed by cranes, not hands. I crushed a few fingers and bloodied my legs, but late that night the pumps were in place, gassed up and pumping water.

Hoses were fed into the spaces and out to the pumps and additional hoses sent the seawater over the side of the transport. The pumps worked all night and divers took turns sleeping, eating and manning the pump controls. Thousands of gallons were sent over the side as the yellow gear worked to beat the leaks from the patches and empty the oil storage compartments.

The Starboard side was emptied faster than the port to correct the list. The plan worked well. By morning the transport was level and the forecastle was above water. The dive team ate peanut butter sandwiches one after another as we worked. The Reclaimer mess crew kept sending more PBJ's and watered down cool aid. I was cold, I ached from sleeping on the steel transport's decks and I longed for a good drink.

The Reclaimer's captain made a few trips over to the transport to check on our progress. Starkey worked through the details of how the vessel would be yanked out of the mud once it was pumped out. Apparently the Pearl Harbor tugs that had placed the oil transport there for sinking had chosen an area that was several yards deep with soft mud. The mud allowed the transport to sink deep, but once raised it was still not free from the muck.

By noon of the second day the transport was above water, but still firmly in the mud of the shallow area. Starkey ordered a meeting on the Reclaimer's mess decks to deal with the beached ship. The master diver laid out the plans on a large white grease pencil board and assigned positions to all the divers in attendance. Removing a beached ship was one of the most complicated and potentially dangerous missions of a salvage vessel like ours. Everyone had to know what they were doing. Every diver had to keep an eye on the rest of the group. A wrong move when pulling thousands of tons could snap cables and cut people in half.

I explained earlier how the Reclaimer actually used physics to tow a ship instead of raw engine power. The inch worm effect of the several ton steel tow cable pulled the vessel in tow along. The same is true for removing ships stuck in mud, sand or on a coral bed. It is not the raw power of the ship that tears free the stricken vessel, once again it involves physics.

The idea was to open the yellow gear storage bays on the fantail and raise out the hydraulic pullers. The pullers were two massive machines that acted much like a crossbow. They were about the size of a small pickup truck and weighed more than just about any other yellow gear on board. Long and black hydraulic lines with stainless steel fittings powered the giant crossbow like devices. They would actually take a strong pull on cables attached to the beached ship.

Being on the water, or underneath, is much like being in space. A diver could not just pull or push on a heavy object and expect it to move. Divers would move instead, and in the opposite direction. For that reason the Reclaimer had to be secured firmly to something before the hydraulic pullers could take a pull on any beached ship. The closest terra firma to the Reclaimer was straight down. The bottom of the ocean, or harbor in this case.

The first step of laying "beach gear", as it was called, was to create a four position pattern with two anchors and two huge steel cables attached to the stricken vessel. Imagine a letter X with the Reclaimer in the middle. The two legs of the X from the aft end, fantail, of the Reclaimer were the anchors the Reclaimer had laid apart and out from the ship about one hundred feet. These secured the Reclaimer to the bottom of the harbor (basically) to allow a strong pull. The top two legs were the two steel cables that went from the hydraulic pullers, through two huge rollers on the Reclaimer's bow and out to the beached vessel.

The Reclaimer was moved into position to drop huge steel cables, about two inches thick, into the water. The cables were coiled in a figure eight fashion on the fantail (back end work area) of the Reclaimer and were slowly fed out to form the back two anchor lines to secure the ship. This was called "laying beach gear".

As the steel cables ran over the side, a loose strand of steel would stick out. The single piece of loose steel fiber would be so sharp and move so fast that a diver's whole palm and fingers would be sliced open right through heavy gloves before they knew it had happened. Divers took turns laying the cables and yes, we all walked away with bleeding hands and legs as tiny steel wires whizzed on by us.

While we were laying the beach gear, one figure eight pattern of cable flipped up unexpectedly and came heading for the four divers holding it and pushing it over the side. Every one watched as the coiled cable slid fast towards the divers. We figured in that split second that it would hit all four of them and take them over the side. With everyone holding their breath, the four guys jumped in the air like four school yard kids playing jump rope and the coil of cable slid under them, slammed into the fantail edge and flipped over the side with a huge splash. We laughed for days about that one, but we sure as hell did not laugh when it happened. And people wonder why salvage divers tend to drink a little after a days work.

With the two lower legs laid out the Reclaimer moved forward to send the two steel cables forward from the ship's bow and out to the oil ransport stuck in the mud. Divers on the fifty foot workboats helped to ferry the cables out and secure them to the transport. The Reclaimer was now in position as the center of the X pattern.

On the Reclaimer's bow the two legs of cable that ran to the transport then fed through the hydraulic pullers that were affixed, hard, to the Reclaimer itself. When the hydraulic pullers took a strong pull on these cables the pull effect along with the weight of the Reclaimer itself in the water, dangling in the center of this X patters, would pull the transport off the mud. That was the physics end of the operation. Once again, physics made up for the Reclaimer's size in a salvage operation.

The power of the hydralic pullers would make them float above the Reclaimer's deck with each strong pull. These pullers were huge and weighed as much as a small armored vehicle. To see them float in the air with the pulls and shake the entire ship showed how powerful they were.

The process of laying beach gear and pulling the transport off the mud took the entire day. We were relived to see the pullers come down to the deck time and time again as the transport slid free. Eventually, the transport was floating in deeper water and the fifty foot workboats from the Reclaimer came along side it to act as tugs and guide it across Pearl Harbor.

We had successfully patched the oil transport's damage, removed it from the beach and taken it to a safe area. The exercise was complete. Each of the dive communities would meet for a barbeque and beers at Alpha docks after the second day. That would end up in a few brawls and fist fights between various divers, the rest would pile into Volkswagen vans and head towards Waikiki to raise hell.

This was what it meant to be a salvage diver. This was the real deal. Raise a sunken ship and yank it off a beachhead. There were no easy days in this job. Divers sweat, hungered and shed blood to get through a day. When it was over I made less than minimum wage and probably spent whatever I had left on cheap beer and steaks for the grill. The saying in the diving navy was "If you ain't salvage, you ain't shit". As miserable as it was, I would take my two years on the Reclaimer over some vacation command any day. If anything, it built character. It also taught me to respect a solid day's work.

The U.S. Naval salvage ship USS Reclaimer ARS 42. Photo is from the coast of Oahu, Hawaii. This photo shows the forward and aft booms used to raise salvage gear from the ship's holds. One 50 foot workboat is missing from it's crane on the starboard side.

The crew of the USS Reclaimer ARS 42 in formation wearing dress white uniforms in Molokai, Hawaii. This view shows the ship's modern forward superstructure that was added to cover the rounded bridge common to ships built during world war two. The 50 foot workboat on the Port side can be clearly seen here as well as the huge rollers on the ship's bow to assist with heavy salvage operations.

Gearing up Mark 12 divers on the USS Reclaimer for deep dive operations. Straps were pulled tight to give more mobility when suit was inflated with air from the dive station compressors.

Divers are fully geared up in Mark 12 suits and helmets. A third diver is set up as an emergency stand-by diver for rescues. Divers can be seen talking into communication microphones and one diver is adjusting air flow.

The fantail of the USS Reclaimer is transformed into a Helium and Oxygen deep dive station with help from Pearl Harbor, Hawaii's Mobile Diving and Salvage unit 1 and their mobile mixed gas dive station equipment. This photo shows the dive staition umbilicals coiled on the decks, the mixed gas operating station and the oxygen scrubers set on each diver's chair attached to a Mark 12 helmet.

Hard at work setting up the Reclaimer's Superlight 17 diving rigs on the fantail. From left to right, Peter, Gordon and Christopher.

The author seated with a Superlight 17 deep sea diving helmet.

A diver wearing the Superlight 17 dive helmet descends a dive station ladder into Pearl Harbor near Alpha docks, home to the USS Reclaimer and Mobile Diving and Salvage Unit 1.

A buddy team of divers wearing the Superlight 17 dive rig are raised off of the deck of dive station and into the ocean using the Reclaimer's aft boom. Master diver Ed Starkey looks on as a first class qualified diver gives boom operation commands as dive station supervisor. Notice how the steel stage is kept steady to prevent mishaps. Divers on the stage keep a wide stance and hold on with both hands.

View of the divers standing on the stage just before being lowered into the water. Notice the dive supervisor watching the stage while giving the command to hold. Another diver is seen with a communication headset.

The USS Reclaimer ties up next to the training vessel used for fire at sea operations. The training ship is an ex-salvage ship from probably WWI or soon after. Some similarities can be seen between the older ship and the fantail of the Reclaimer such as the huge "H" bits used to tie up ships in distress. Master diver Starkey is seen standing on the training vessel barking commands.

Oil transport in Pearl Harbor shown after Navy SEAL team members detonated charges below the water line. Now it is up to the Reclaimer divers to patch and raise the vessel.

Salvage pumps from the Reclaimer are used to remove water from the oil transport's holds after damages were temporarily patched.

Divers from the Reclaimer tend to the salvage pumps as headway is made. Heavy corrosion is already visible even after a few days of the oil transport being below the water.

Master diver Ed Starkey walks along the oil transport's catwalk to survey the progress.

The oil transport takes on a bad list while it slowly rises from the harbor mud.

Chapter 7
Rescue at sea.

The barracks on Pearl Harbor were slowly being renovated and older structures were being removed all together during the early nineties. Three large barracks buildings were in need of demolition, but without funds the Navy decided to leave them. Instead the smaller ships stationed at Pearl were allowed to put some single sailors in the rooms. No ship was smaller than the USS Reclaimer. I put in my paperwork to be relocated in the old barracks facilities and get off the ship. It worked out well as several divers and I were moved to the buildings.

The married sailors on the Reclaimer could always go home at the end of the day, but the single sailors were new to the idea of actually leaving the ship after a days work and driving home. For so long we were living in the tiny deck department bunk room. It was the only home we had known. Almost thirty persons in a shoebox for years. Heck, sailors had lived like that on the Reclaimer for decades.

On a Sunday morning I was asleep in my rickety double bunk in the new Reclaimer barracks. It was about three in the morning and dark out. Every window was kept permanently open as the humidity was terrible and it was not as if I owned anything worth stealing. Most of us did not even lock our doors. My life's possessions consisted of a few tattered aloha shirts and a warm case of cheap beer. If some burglar was that desperate to steal something from me, they could have it. Hopefully they would have the common decency of leaving a can or two for when I woke up.

The whole building was dark and quiet from the weekend of barbeques. Each room on a Friday and Saturday night would pump music loud and the courtyard between the barracks structures were lively with sizzling steaks, cold beer and general mayhem. By this time, Sunday morning, I was spent and just trying to get some sleep for the new week.

My sleep was cut short when the squeal of a fan belt and the grinding of bad brakes woke me up. Some old military vehicle had rumbled its way up to the front of our barracks. Seconds later the driver began to lay on the horn over and over waking the whole damn building up. Tired, hung over and now pissed off I walked to the railings and began to scream obscenities at the driver to stop and go away. He would not.

The driver stepped out of the old gray passenger van and walked up to the courtyard. He was wearing the familiar blue dungaree uniform of the a navy enlisted man. The young sailor put his hands up to block several empty beer bottles and cans flying at him from various locations on the barrack's railings. Still he fought his way into the courtyard and put his hands to his mouth to call out.

"Reclaimer! Reclaimer sailors! Get down here now! Its an emergency!" He screamed out to all of us.

We stopped and listened to what he was saying. We were after all a vessel that was primarily used for rescue work. We just were not used to getting called out for it. The young man shouted once more.

"Reclaimer sailors! You have to get to your ship, get down here now! There is no time to get ready! Just come!" He waved to his van and ran back towards the parking lot.

This guy meant business. I grabbed my boots and a pair of coveralls and headed for the stairwells. I ran in my boxer shorts and bare feet for the vehicle. A few guys were pounding on doors to wake up those who were still crashed in their beds.

Something or someone was having a bad day and the closest deep water rescue ship in the Pacific Ocean was generally the Reclaimer. The crew scrambled down to the van and piled inside. There was only enough seats for about six guys so we literally piled on top of each other until we had about twenty guys packed inside. The driver backed out and tore away from the barracks heading for the Reclaimer tied up at Alpha Docks.

It was still dark and quiet on Pearl Harbor as our dangerously overloaded van sped through the streets. The morning commuters would start coming through the Pearl harbor gates about five or six in the morning. Thank God. The way we were driving we would have no doubt broad sided another vehicle had it been any later in the morning.

Twisting around corners we came dangerously close to tipping as we made our way across the base. The guys inside held on to each other as the van's doors were strained from the crowded cabin. The driver stayed focused on the road and steered like a madman to keep us from taking curbs, street signs and mailboxes.

We arrived at the ship to find the overnight watch had already fired up the diesels and black smoke was pouring out from the Reclaimer's exhaust stack. There were a few people running around the ship's decks, but it was the fact that every one of the ship's exterior lights were lit that gave it away the Reclaimer was   pulling out soon.

Once on board I ran to my duty station at a port side line to get the ship underway. The engines were pumping hard in the lower spaces and the whole ship vibrated from the testing of the screws and rudders. The ship lurched forward and then back as the gear reduction units and the reverse gear boxes were given last minute run downs.

The emergency was not yet known to me. I was being told to start throwing the lines over the side in order to get underway. The married sailors were not even at the ship yet. The captain was in such a hurry that he figured the skeleton crew of single sailors would have to get the job done.

Luckily a few married sailors began to run up to the ship and climb aboard just as we were getting ready to throw the aluminum walkway, or gangplank, onto the pier to save time from having to heave it onboard.

One of the arriving crew members yelled out that Master Diver Starkey was right behind him. Walking towards the ship from the darkness was the lumbering shape of Master Diver Starkey. As soon as he stepped foot on the ship the gang plank went flying and the last lines were tossed off. The Captain was on board and yelling orders both from the microphone system and over the side at the deck sailors.

As the Reclaimer began to back away from the pier a Navy panel truck showed up full of canned food and bread. The sailors in the truck were actually throwing the bread and canned goods onto our ship as we pulled away. They tossed full cases at first and individual loaves and cans when we were too far away. It was a crazy sight.

The captain had the Reclaimer turn sharp when it entered the harbor passage and shifted into forward with a powerful lurch. The Reclaimer shuttered as the screws spun faster than the ship was moving forward. We gained speed until we were at max and headed out for open water.

I turned and watched as Pearl Harbor disappeared behind me. On the pier at Alpha Docks several sailors who had not arrived soon enough watched the Reclaimer pull out. Other sailors were there as well and they just starred at us until we were out of sight in the darkness of open ocean. It was about three thirty in the morning and the black, Pacific night swallowed us up.

The crew were covering for empty duty stations as the morning light began to arrive over the horizon. Deck department sailors brought new lines up from the ship's storage holds to replace those that were thrown over the side in haste. Afterwards the "deck apes" were assigned to take over empty engine and operations posts.

I was certified to do about three or four different non deck related watches including Sounding and Security (you all remember how much fun that watch was), control panel in engineering and manning the wheel on the bridge. I crossed through the mess decks to grab a cardboard box full of sandwiches and warm cans of cola to take up to the bridge. I ate while I steered the ship. The crew was still not being told what this was all about.

It was nothing new to be kept in the dark about operations until a sailor was actually in need of knowing. That was standard procedure in the Navy. Just do the job an figure that someone had the big picture. I, of course, hated that and usually found ways to get information. On a ship the size of the Reclaimer it was not long before I knew what was up.

Apparently a cargo ship was on its way towards the middle east with about fifty M-1 Abrahms main battle tanks on board, getting ready for something big. The movement of such a massive force was being kept under wraps until whatever the pentagon was planning had started. For that reason the Reclaimer crew was the only group to know this cargo vessel was even on the ocean.

When the tank transport ship was a solid days journey from any land mass the engines decided to shut down and now it was drifting in the Pacific Ocean. It was basically unable to control its movement in any way and the seas were getting rougher as the hours went by. On board the transport had about a half billion dollars worth of the world's most sophisticated and deadly tanks.

The tank transport was a civilian cargo vessel which gave it a quiet and un-military look from the outside. When the Reclaimer arrived within visual distance I could see the transport was taking hard rolls in the rough ocean. The weight of its cargo was giving the transport good ballast, but it also increased the likely hood of capsizing if we did not get the vessel under way. The journey to the transport ship had taken the Reclaimer all day. Hours of rough ocean cruising in our tiny vessel. Most of the Reclaimer's crew were either sick from the ride or from the drinking the days before, but by god we made it there.

The Reclaimer had rescued military ships before. Hawaii has a capable civilian rescue vessel kept up by the state, but in military matters the Navy liked to utilize it's own resources and keep the press quiet. In the Pacific arena the Reclaimer was the designated rescue and salvage ship. We could be called out to just about anywhere at a moments notice. Tahiti, Guam, the Philippine Islands. The Reclaimer was not fast, but it carried enough fuel to get to just about anywhere in the Pacific. When the Reclaimer was sent out for a rescue it carried equipment to do just about anything that might come along.

One of the Reclaimer's first missions when I got on board was to assist a navy vessel about two hours out from Pear Harbor. This had been a hush, hush type operation at first. The Reclaimer was called out early in the day and headed for the area of the stricken ship.

This time we were at full crew and considered it to be a regular work mission. The Pearl harbor command called our homes and families to tell them we were not coming home that night because of an emergency. The trip would turn out to be anything but a regular operation.

The Reclaimer arrived at the location of the vessel about noon and found no ship in distress. Instead there was a Navy destroyer cruising slowly towards us from what we believed to be the location of the ship in trouble. The huge destroyer cruised up to our little rescue-diving vessel and blocked us from continuing forward.

The captains of our ship and the destroyer talked over the radio for several hours. I eventually learned that the ship in distress was not a ship at all, but a submarine that had lowered its anchors in shallow waters during an operation, submerged. The sub was not able to bring the anchors up and, thus, was stuck at about a depth of twenty feet with it's anchor chain dangling down into the ocean. It was an embarrassing situation, as you can imagine, for the submarine captain.

The navy sent out the destroyer to keep other ships away while the Reclaimer made it's way to the area. Now they expected master diver Starkey to come up with a solution. The Navy would not accept a nuclear attack submarine stuck with an non-retracting chain problem. The Pearl harbor submarine admirals wanted our captain to get that submarine moving again fast and not attract attention to the operation. Enter the problem solver, Starkey.

This was one of those bizarre situations that a salvage diving vessel could find itself in. The Navy considers ARS ships to be problem solvers. The Reclaimer was basically designed to do anything from blowing up sunken ships that blocked harbors in a time of war to raising lost vessels and then towing them to a friendly port. The ARS was the "get the job done" ship of the fleet and it was not uncommon to find the Reclaimer in a situation that did not come with a procedure manual. This was one of those situations.

Not to sound stupid here, I did not realize that submarines even used their anchors while submerged. I knew they had them as I had performed hull checks on nuclear submarines now and then when the divers at the Pearl Harbor Submarine Base Dive Locker would ask for some extra help. The closest dive commands would send a few divers over for the week to make up for guys who may have been on vacation or sick leave.

When I heard that the submarine had lowered its anchor to hold itself in position while submerged I was confused. I guess it made sense, I mean the sub would not want to drift around while it was submerged, it could strike a rock on the bottom. I just never thought about it.

Master Diver Starkey spent the day in the radio room talking with the captains of all three ships. Starkey a plan to raise the sub's anchor that he figured would work and would not raise eyebrows in the area. The easy way of doing this was to just cut the stinking chain and let the submarine go back to port. What was a chain worth in comparison to a billion dollar attack sub? The Reclaimer divers could always go down and retrieve the chain later if need be. That idea was quick and dirty, but the submarine's captain did not like the idea of any type of cutting torch being used around his vessel's hull. I guess the guy had a point.

Master Diver Starkey called a meeting of the divers on board down in the Reclaimer's dive locker. We drew several ideas on our white grease pencil board and argued about the feasibility of each operation. Finally Starkey decided we needed to get started and came up with a simple plan.

The fantail of the Reclaimer was set up for dive station and the divers were geared up to go in about an hour. The salvage supply locker had about four chain falls that could handle heavy loads. These were massive chain falls that were intended to move around yellow gear if the ship's booms were inoperative. It took two people to get them around the ship because the chain falls were so heavy. In the water, though, they could be moved easier.

The idea was to go about one quarter of the way down on the chain and pass a heavy length of steel line through one of the links. On each end would be a secured loop. This was called a "strap". The Reclaimer carried dozens of straps in all sizes to do various jobs. Once in place the chain fall would be extended out to the cable and the lowest quarter of the anchor chain would be raised from the bottom.

The second chain fall would be used to raise the next quarter of anchor chain. By then the submarine could get free and make it's way to the surface. With the chain still drooping from the submarine's hull it could head back to Pearl Harbor for repairs.

The plan had never been tried, usual for the salvage navy, but it worked on paper. The chain falls were rated to handle the weight involved (sort of). The cables were within their limits as well (according to the manufacturers). The Reclaimer divers had used chain falls underwater before for various jobs so it all seemed to make sense.

Of course the ship's captains thought it was a confused mess. The mental pictures Starkey drew for them did not help. Our captain convinced the other two that Starkey's idea was the fastest feasible way to solve the situation before nightfall. With trepidation the chain fall plan was agreed upon and the Reclaimer began to set up dive station.

The experience of slowly descending on the nuclear submarine in the clear blue Pacific water is one I will always remember. The dive team covered the entire length of the sub's hull to ensure the chain was the only issue we were dealing with. After a complete hull inspection I dove along the length of anchor chain to the anchor itself to free any debris that may prevent the chain falls from raising it.

The sub's anchor retrieval system was the problem here, not the anchor being fouled. I described the situation and the condition of the anchor equipment to Master Diver Starkey on the dive station. In about an hour my dive buddy and I were rigging the first steel straps to the lower links of anchor chain and above another two divers were attaching the first huge chain fall. The day was rolling along fine, but the night was coming and we had to get this sub free and moving.

With the chain fall extended to allow it to hook onto our steel strap, my dive buddy and I pulled on the chain fall's raising and lowering chain. Let me explain this clearer. A chain fall is basically a gear reduction unit. A long chain is attached to one wheel. As a diver spins the wheel by pulling on the first chain, a series of gears spin a second wheel about twelve inches away at a slower rate. The second wheel also has tremendous lift capability. Attached to the second wheel is a long chain with a hook at one end. It was World War One technology that still worked just fine today. The chain fall, god's gift to the salvage navy.

Chain falls were easy enough to operate above water, but underwater I faced the zero gravity type situation I explained earlier. As I pulled on the first chain, I would go upwards as much as I tried to pull the chail down.

To pull a heavy load I had to be secured to something to operate the chain fall underwater.

One diver held the other as well as the anchor chain itself to give the support base needed to yank on the first chain. The anchor slowly came free from the bottom and it would seem Starkey's idea was a success. We pulled up the first chain fall until Master Diver Starkey had new divers rig the second. The weight increased in the second pull, but the operation was already coming to an end. The excitement of having solved the problem and freeing the submarine gave the divers the energy needed to bring up the anchor chain and let the sub head for Pearl Harbor.

The Submarine drifted away from the other ships, surfaced and started for port as we broke down dive station on the Reclaimer. It would be well after dark that the Reclaimer would tie up at alpha docks and hose down the ship with fresh water. Each rescue operation came with its own challenges. The crew could not really prepare for them, we just had to be ready to think on the fly.

The Reclaimer closed the distance with the huge civilian cargo ship that carried the M1 Abrams tanks. The heavy seas rolled both of our vessels forward, back and side to side. Standing on the decks was dangerous and I held on to rails or pipes to keep my footing. The wind and waves told the me it was only going to get worse out here. The captain figured any move the Reclaimer was going to make had better go down now.

At a distance of around three hundred feet the Reclaimer's divers launched a small inflatable boat with an engineering team to work on the transport ship's problems. The team from the Reclaimer grabbed onto a waving rope ladder that the cargo ship's deck crew had lowered to them. I was working the bow of the inflatable boat that transported the engine team over. I watched as they, one by one, waited for the seas to raise the inflatable boat up to the ladder, grabbed hold and climbed up. Once one team member would grab the rope ladder, the seas would drop and so would the inflatable boat below them. It was quite a sight and thank God no one fell off the ladder.

Master Diver Starkey reasoned that weather the team got the transport ship's engines working again or not shouldn't prevent the Reclaimer from towing it closer to Pearl Harbor. The seas were bad enough and he wanted to have the cargo ship under tow before it got worse out there.

An M-1 rifle was used to launch a small orange line over to the cargo ship from the Reclaimer's fantail and across their bow. The sailors on board the transport pulled it in. Attached to the light line was a standard ship's mooring line that the Relciamer divers extended over to the stranded ship's crew. In turn, this was tied to a huge hawser line. The kind that could pull tremendous loads. The hawser was the final length to send over and we attached it to the H bits on the Reclaimer's fantail. The cargo ship's crew worked with the Reclaimer sailors that transferred over to their side and secured the hawser to the bow of the transport.

While the engineering crew worked in the lower spaces of the cargo ship, the Reclaimer's divers took a slow but firm pull on the hawser line until we had the vessel in a slow tow. The Reclaimer must have been doing no more than three or four knots, but at least we were making headway for Pearl Harbor. By night fall the engineering team gave up on the cargo ship's engines and ate dinner on board instead of trying to transfer back to the Reclaimer in the dark.

To the average fishing boat passing by as we made for the mouth of Pearl Harbor, it appeared that the Reclaimer was towing a cargo ship full of just about any worthless junk back to port. The reality that the transport was carrying a battle group of tremendous proportions, going god only knows where or why, was hidden. The Reclaimer handed the cargo vessel off to two military tugs from Pearl Harbor just outside of the Harbor itself and returned to Alpha Docks.

A tour on a salvage ship will bring a half dozen such rescues or salvage operations every year. Salvage ships have retrieved lost fighter jets, civilian airliners and even the space shuttle Challenger after it disintegrated over the Florida Coast. Salvage ship crews generally get no praise or recognition for their efforts, but because of the navy salvage diving fleet the rest of the military moves along smoothly. Salvage ships pull off the missions no one else wants or knows how to do.

The reward was a torn muscle or two in my lower back and perhaps a few good memories. No action packed movies, no heroes, no shiny medals. Salvage sailors just got the damn job done when we were called out to do it.

Chapter 8
Missions, visions and excursions.

The crew of the Reclaimer was constantly trained on rescue and salvage ideas. To assist in the training an old salvage vessel, from pre WWII, was maintained at Alpha Docks, Pearl Harbor, to be used as a "stricken vessel". The old and rusted hulk was tied up beside the USS Reclaimer most of time, only to be towed out to open ocean for ship to ship fire and rescue exercises.

I often looked over at the older salvage ship and wondered how it was to be stationed on it in those early Navy years. The 1920's or 30's. The accommodations must have been even worse than on the Reclaimer. I think salvage sailors expected it, opposed to today's sailors who see advertisements of high tech navy ships and carriers cruising the world's oceans. When a young man is stationed on the Reclaimer he first asks himself if he did something wrong or pissed someone off in his last command. The sailors who stood watch on the old salvage boat we used for training probably expected the harsh realities of the salvage navy and were damn glad to have a paycheck in those times of the Great depression.

The aft section of the training vessel had a large steel box mounted on it to be filled with scrap wood and set aflame. It simulated an onboard fire that ships like ours would encounter on the open ocean. The idea was to get close, put out the flames with our powerful water cannons on board and eventually board the ship for rescue actions. The closer to reality the Relciamer could train the better.

The two years I was onboard the USS Reclaimer would bring, of course, a fire-rescue drill. Master diver Starkey discussed the mission at length with the various deck and diving departments on board in the mess hall. Charts and diagrams were laid out to explain how, in a perfect world, the Reclaimer would approach and begin to extinguish the gasoline fueled flames rising from the training ship's fantail.

Each member of the crew knew how they would play a role in a major rescue action. Deck and diving divisions would take the lead with actually fighting fires and boarding the ship in distress. The engineering and operations staff would maintaining water pressures, ship's positions and communications. All were needed to not only complete the mission, but to get the divers who would board the training ship back alive.

The Relciamer's dive team tied up the old, rusted training ship to our aft "H" bits using strong hawser line like the one we towed the stricken cargo ship in with. The rusted ship made for dangerous work. Cuts required tetanus shots from the Reclaimer's corpsmen (medical staff). There was always a handful of hornets nests that had formed over the months that the training ship sat unused at Alpha docks. The interior decks were rusted and could give way under the weight of anyone walking on them sending a sailor crashing to the level below.

The divers were, as usual, used as the direct contact crew with the old salvage vessel because of these kinds of dangers. The navy used divers as the dogs of the fleet. It did not necessarily matter if a job had to be carried out underwater, it just had to be miserable. For that reason, divers were paid a stipend every month above our dismal navy enlisted pay. Called "diving pay", the extra income almost perfectly paid for a twelve pack of beer and a bag of pretzels per day. The navy knew just how to take care of us.

After a few hours of securing the training ship to side of the Reclaimer, the dive team stationed ourselves on the fantail of the Reclaimer in case a tow line began to give way. Not that we would have a lot of options in such a case. When a line securing a two ships together begins to fray and snap apart, the emergency action prescribed is to run like hell.

The idea was to move both ships out side by side until the Relciamer could actually take the training ship under tow. The lighter lines that secured the two vessels together were always under stress and could "snap-back." A term that described this dangerous situation very well.

Carefully, the Reclaimer made it's way out of the mouth of Pearl Harbor and placed the training ship in tow. The Reclaimer would tow it out far enough to set it afire and not alarm the dozens of fishing vessels that cruised the coast lines of Hawaii every day. Most likely we would take it just beyond the horizon, about twenty miles or so.

Underway, the Reclaimer crew would spend the days tossing fishing lines off the fantail ourselves and playing various games like ring toss. The off going watches would converge for bar-b-que and a game of ring toss while music played from a boom box tied to the aft superstructure. Salvage duty was rough in the navy and any attempt to lighten our spirits was usually supported by the captain.

One classic trip to Molokai, a small island near Oahu, The crew was given a few days to head out and see the island. As the Reclaimer pulled into port, the captain had the crew dress out in our white navy uniforms and present ourselves in an official manner for the Molokai population. Molokai was almost never visited by navy ships as the port was too shallow. The Reclaimer was designed to enter shallow areas and work more inland if need be. The idea of a navy ship pulling in to port excited the island residents and all the schools turned out to take the children on tours of the Reclaimer. Even the local high school band played on the docks and a Hula dancing group danced for the crew as we tied up. In our dress whites the Reclaimer crew lined the dock. It was a fun trip for the island and the ship's crew.

The Reclaimer, being rather small and only requiring a minor crew to maintain while in port, was for the most part shut down and only a skeleton crew left on board. The divers and deck apes divided up to head out to Molokai's diverse cultural environment (one bar, PauHana's, and a convenience store).

I set up a group to hike a little known state trail that had been closed due to over growth and lack of upkeep. The Wailau trail, it was a true Hawaii hike that only a small group on board would want to undertake. We set off, about five of us, with back packs, sleeping bags and enough beer to get us through. Luckily Molokai is small enough where anyone walking along the road is quickly picked up by a passing pickup truck. We were given a lift by some locals to the head of the trail.

The trail head was in an unpopulated stretch of Molokai's road ways. Most of Molokai, to be honest, is unpopulated, so we did not expect to find a gift shop or anything. We set up our sleeping bags and broke out some booze to enjoy the rest of the cool island day.

A visitor wandered into our camp and stayed with us for the trip. A tan and pink colored dog that had no identification. The dog was tame and relaxed with our group soon earning itself the nickname of "the mad dog of Molokai". We drank and talked story through the day.

As dusk began to approach the camp area, I called the other four divers into the woodlands around us, toward the trail. I pushed my way through the heavy foliage until I came upon our friend, standing next to a huge stone structure about twelve feet high. It was a Heiau, or Hawaiian burial mound. Molokai was the burial place for thousands of ancient Hawaiians who built these magnificent mounds to cover the dead.

The mound was a true feat of workmanship. It stood twelve feet high, at least a football field long and twenty five to thirty feet wide. The heiau was built of dark gray lava rocks about one to two feet in diameter. The overgrowth of the jungle had covered it so well I did not notice that our camp site was directly next to it. It was too late to move as the darkness was fast approaching so we took a few last photos of the amazing mound and made our way back to camp.

That night I made a pot of coffee with my small camp stove and talked about the burial mound that was just passed the woods edge from us. It's size and design gave it an appearance of great importance. Perhaps kings and great leaders were buried there. There was room in the structure to hold thousands of Hawaiian's bones during those early, pre-Cooke discovery years. The heiau made for quiet and respectful conversation as we drifted off to sleep.

That night we each had dreams about the mound. Our group had discussed it up until we went to sleep which could have attributed to this fact, but I will never forget the realistic nature of my dream in particular. Even today, years later, I can remember the dream clearly.

In my dream it was day again and I sat in our camp, with the rest of our group sleeping in their bags. Only the mad dog himself was awake and sitting across the camp from me. As I sat there I watched dozens of traditionally dressed Hawaiian natives wander through our camp. The visitors would stop to look at me with puzzled faces and questioning looks. The Hawaiians passing through pointed to me and looked at each other as if to ask if anyone knew who I was and why I was sitting there. They did not speak.

Adult women and men, middle aged, elderly and even children walked passed me as I sat transfixed and unable to move. I was fully aware of them and they of me, yet I could not talk or move. I am not sure I would have even if I could. I remember one middle aged woman in particular who acted as if she knew the dog and greeted it. She and the dog looked over at me and she had the same look as if to ask why I was there. She was dressed in bright colored cloth and had dark and thick hair flowing over her shoulders. She was quite beautiful. Eventually she walked directly over to me and leaned over as to put her face very close to mine. She examined me and my clothing closely. She then stood back up and walked back into the woods with a few glances at me as she walked away.

The other distinct memory was of two children, one boy and one girl about three or four years old. They played in the camp with each other and paid no attention to me. They patted the mad dog a few times on the head and ran off into the woods as the image eventually faded and I went back to sleep.

The next morning each of our group who had slept in the camp slowly began to discuss our various memories and dreams of the night before. Most of our group spoke about just flashing images and could not remember detailed information. Or at least they did not want to talk about it. My story was far too detailed to give in full at that moment so I went along with the rest in saying that I too had seen a few odd things in my dreams as well.

With that we packed up and began our way up the Wailau State trail. A trek that would take most of the day to get up and back. The views from the top of the Molokai mountains were incredible. The majestic island stretched out in both directions from our trail. The cool ocean winds blew against us and stayed with us as we made our way back down the mountain side.

Our friend the dog was not there for the journey along the trail. He was not in our camp when we awoke and started out. The Mad Dog of Molokai. I guess he had other matters to attend to that day. He was just one of the memories not to be forgotten from my trip to Molokai.

The Reclaimer staged the training ship with a full load of wood dowsed in gasoline. The divers set the wood pile afire and the captain took the Reclaimer further away to simulate closing in on the vessel while engulfed in flame. The Reclaimer's water cannons worked well to knock down the fires as we came closer to the burning old salvage ship. Each of the Reclaimer's two water cannons sent a steady a nd powerfull stream of seawater over to the wood fires as we brought our vessel closer and prepared to board.

Hand held fire hoses were laid out and prepared to be passed over to divers when they boarded the burning ship. Our group donned fire gear and OBA's, Oxygen Breathing Apparatus. When the two ships were side by side, the training ship slamming into the Reclaimer with the force of the deep ocean waves behind it, our group climbed over the side and set up a fire station on the fantail of the older ship.

Master Diver Starkey never liked to supervise from a distance and made his way over to the blazing fantail as well. He barked orders to the rest of the divers getting our group ready to move forward with hoses and engage the fire head on. Starkey had seen real fires on ships in his years of experience on board salvage ships. The Master Diver's most frequent command was to just pull our heads out of our asses as he watched us turn our back to the flames or position ourselves in a dangerous area. I could imagine he had lost crew members in fire fights over his career and knew what he was talking about.

Hoses, extra OBA canisters and other heavy rescue gear was handed over to us and we began to make our way towards the flames. The old salvage ship bobbed in the ocean violently throwing us off our balance. The hand held hose systems were powerful and required several guys on each to bend them around for use. A mixture of soap foam and water was used as the gasoline fire could re-ignite if it was able to keep contact with Oxygen. The foam created a layer that blocked O2 from meeting the hot wood and fuel.

An hour or so was spent to knock out the flames on the main deck. The gasoline smell and black smoke made the operation a hell-like environment. With the outside decks secured well enough, the dive moved the hoses deeper into the training ship. The team went through the motions of clearing the spaces on board just as we would in a real fire on the seas situation. Each space on board had to be checked and the information passed up to the supervisor. The master diver would in turn keep the Reclaimer's crew and captain advised.

Inside the training ship the smoke and heat burned my eyes and skin even with the protective gear on. Each space I entered had old steel equipment mounted to the decks. I could not see the obstacles in front of me, I just sort of crashed into them as I felt my way forward. When I reached one of the interior bins used to light the wood and gasoline fires, my team would hose it down with water and foam until it was out. The fire team and I went from room to room this way.

Supervisors called out for reports as we progressed. The old salvage vessel took its revenge on several members of the team. Bruises and cuts added to the heat and smoke. After another hour inside the training ship the interior fires were out. We began to back ourselves and our equipment from the spaces.

Our crew that worked on the old salvage boat was tired and covered in soot. I stripped down to my tan dive shorts and began to clean the Reclaimer's rescue gear. Hoses and OBA's were washed and passed back to the Reclaimer. The Reclaimer's deck department crew tied the older vessel tight to the Reclaimer's side to subside the violent slamming action that was occurring on the open ocean. By the end of the day the dive team had the old, burnt wood cleaned up and the Reclaimer's gear stowed in its place.

Master Diver Starkey debriefed the crew and captain in an after action report on the Reclaimer's mess decks. He discussed our problems and mistakes. As always the divers improvised as the training exercise moved along. It was the way of the salvage navy. There were no definitive guide books or training manuals that could cover the missions a salvage ship would encounter. The very nature of the salvage/diving world was to undertake missions that were not clear, or easily handled.

The salvage navy was always training for emergencies on the high seas. Lost submarines, beached ships, vessels in trouble during storms. I was guided by the experience master diver Starkey brought to the table.

The rest of the Reclaimer's crew would move from ship to ship as their navy careers continued. This was not so true for the divers, diving supervisors and master diver. Once assigned to a salvage command divers would often go from ship salvage to shore salvage duties, keeping the knowledge they acquired within the community.

Master diver Starkey was even held back from retiring twice during my time working with him due to the lack of experience other salvage master divers had within the Pacific Arena. The navy went as far as to create a master diver specialty in salvage and sent the first few candidates to Starkey to work under him in Hawaii for a year or so. Only then was he able to retire.

Salvage divers who are later transferred to "kinder, gentler" commands often deal with a confusing transition. The work no longer entails buckets of grease and hours of welding steel plates together. Non salvage diving commands are clean, and well laid out. This is a big change from the industrial and construction atmosphere of a salvage command.

The shore based Mobile Diving and Salvage Unit 1 diving command, housed at the Alpha Docks facility alongside the Reclaimer, was a classic salvage diving command. The arrangement of warehouses and work spaces were based on needs and not esthetics. Buildings of various sizes and shapes were erected as commanders wanted additional storage, welding and fabrication workshops.

Salvage ships were no different. "Junk Boats" were constructed around the equipment they carried. Once designers had placed the towing, hauling, lifting hardware they blocked off most the remaining room on board to carry salvage gear, yellow gear, steel cables and diving air compressors. Anything that was left was converted into berthing and mess decks.

I am not joking about this. The Reclaimer had huge spaces devoted to storing yellow gear with good air conditioning and lighting. The crew, however, slept in oddball, wedge shaped spaces with low overheads. Dozens of sailors slept in cramped spaces no larger than a closet while steel cable was coiled in rooms large enough to play racquetball in.

Prison-like living conditions and dangerous work, that was my two year tour on a salvage ship in the United States Navy. Afterwards I could live just about anywhere and do any miserable job out there and not be discouraged. They told me it would build character. Well, most divers were strange characters to start out with. Two years on a salvage boat like the Reclaimer was like graduate school for the hopelessly nuts.

One afternoon I was called into the Reclaimer's Captain's cabin with another diver on board named Brian Baxter. Brian was an intelligent and outdoors minded man who had a few more years on him than most of the second class divers on board. He had a great sense of humor and a cynical side that kept us all laughing.

The captain told Baxter and I that he wanted us to represent the Reclaimer in a joint operation that was being put together at the Pearl Harbor command. Two sailors from the salvage boat and two from the navy base would join army soldiers and marines to Kohoolawe island and help remove ordinance that may obstruct the island's rejuvenation program.

Let me explain. Kahoolawe had been used as a military bomb target for about four decades and was just now getting handed back to the Hawaiian people. It was off the coast of Maui and Lanai. Kahoolawe island needed years of deep digging and ordinance disposal work before Hawaiians would ever be able to live and farm there again.

The first step of the clean up was to insure that civilian contractors who would work on the island would not accidentally step on a live bomb or missile and get killed. The insurance and law suit pay out would be costly. The answer was to line un a hundred enlisted military personnel and walk us across the fields and sand to ensure no live munitions were still floating around.

Military personnel could not sue the service and, I guess, I knew I might get killed when I enlisted, Right? The use of soldiers and sailors was, economically, the right decision. Brian and I agreed to go because we both liked to hike outer island in Hawaii. We had covered almost every island and the captain knew the two of us would want to go to Kahoolawe.

We loaded up a sea bag with two weeks of coveralls and underwear and headed for the Marine base in Kaneohe Hawaii, the other side of Oahu from Honolulu and Pearl Harbor Naval Base. Once there Baxter and I were loaded onto twin engine helicopters along side about a hundred other poor bastards that got talked into the mission. The helicopters, about four of them, started up and we were off for Kahoolawe.

The flight was great as the helicopters did not gain any real altitude. The older Vietnam era helicopters were slow and stayed low enough to give us a good look of the island as we traversed the Pacific Ocean. Baxter and I crossed over Oahu and head towards Molokai. From there we turned towards Kahoolawe and crossed between Lanai and Maui. The view of the islands at this altitude was worth the trip alone.

Once on island, we were given instruction to find a bunk n one of the five or six steel half moon shaped huts that had been on Kahoolawe since the end of world war two. The huts were good enough for Brian and I as we were used to tents when we traveled. The idea of having three meals a day prepared for us and actual showers to use at night was a luxury.

The huts and a few warehouses were built by the navy in the 1940's to house a unit of Seabees on Kahoolawe. Seabees were the navy's heavy construction battalions (C.B.'s) . The Seabees were the only residents on the island for the decades of bombing that occurred there. Now the Seabees were gone and we were getting their old facilities.

The command did not care if we wore uniforms or civilian clothes while we worked. It was going to be about two weeks of tough walking and hauling metal fragments. The best outfit was military pants and boots with a light civilian shirt and hat. The idea was to stay cool on the island.

Kahoolawe is a dry and dead place. There are only dead trees and rocks to break up the sand and gravel. Huge bomb craters littered the surface like the moon's asteroid craters. The rains had no where to go as there was no vegetation to soften the grounds. The rain waters would flood quickly and rush off the island's surface to the sea in powerful rivers of mud.

Brian and I found a couple of bunks in one of the huts and set up our area. We grabbed something to eat in the mess hall and wandered out to muster up at around noon. The operation was headed up by the navy's Explosive Ordinance Disposal divers or EOD teams. That is why they wanted a few navy representatives to go along with the soldiers. Lucky us.

We were explained to that the operation had a goal to collect metal fragments from the surface of the dirt and sand. This, according to the EOD personnel, would clear the way for further excavation and ordinance removal. It was, of course, total bull. One inch under the sand would be another full layer of shrapnel and bomb fragments. They wanted us to believe that clearing only what the eye can see would make it safe for heavier work teams to come in? This was a joke.

The real reason was that if our group could walk over the sand without dying it was safe enough to bring in civilians to actually get some real clean up work done. The EOD team was smart though. They set up a competition between the Army and Marines to see who could cover the most ground, in a line up, and remove the most scrap metal.

Soldiers were always up for a competition, especially one between services. The few navy guys joined the Marine side and we were off. We loaded up in old one tone Army trucks and rumbled off to the target zones. I had to keep from laughing about how screwed up the whole situation was. Brian and I did not think that the other soldiers even knew what was really going on here. No need to say anything that might hurt moral, so we just shut up and went along.

The trucks had a hard time moving through the deep mud rivers and eroded gullies. We spent as much time off the tucks pushing and working metal pry bars as we did ridding in the back. There were about five actual Vietnam era army jeeps on the island that were in working condition. The jeeps drove along with us as well and had just as hard a time. It was cool to operate the old military vehicles though.

After an hour of hard riding and pushing we arrived at the first site we would clean. One of the army trucks was converted into a dump truck and would hold our scrap metal. The EOD team had us line up and stretch across the landscape. Our one hundred or so strong clean up crew made for a good line. We handed out canvas bags and buckets to hold the scrap metal and started our day.

The idea was not to get ahead of the two people on the ends of the line. As we walked we picked up scrap fragments of bombs and missiles fired from fighter jets into the targets that used to be erected…right where we were friggin' walking! All of a sudden this did not seem so cool any more.

As I walked I overheard the soldiers cheer and shout as they found larger and larger fragments of old ordinance to add to their team's load. Most of the bombs were blown into pieces the size of soft balls so you spent a lot of time bent over and scooping the junk up. Brian and I would gather some metal fragments and chat with each other about how we would be lucky to make it two weeks walking around a damn bomb field.

The EOD guys would make sure plenty of water was handed out and we all carried old canteens and web belts. It was nice that they were so concerned about our welfare. After all, it would be a shame if one of us passed out from heat exhaustion while we were clearing a field of unexploded 1000 pound incendiary bombs.

I was about two hours into the operation when I spotted a spike shaped piece of shrapnel. It looked a lot like a star shape or something you would mix with in the kitchen. I reached down an yanked at it to toss in my metal bucket. It did not want to budge.

I pulled out a piece of scrap metal from my bucket and used it to dig around the strange object in hope of freeing it from the compacted dry sand. Attached to the star shaped metal tip was the familiar rounded body of a bomb, a big bomb. I had no idea how large it was as the roundness of it just kept going wider and wider. I figure this may be a good time to get someone's attention.

I waved over am EOD diver who looked down at the object. Trying not to show his concern he stammered out " O.K. Ill flag it, walk around it and keep going." What? Keep going? Hello, Earth to bomb dude. Was this thing going to go off or something?

The EOD guy stuck a little red flag on a metal wire next to the bomb and made some marks into his wire bound notebook. I looked at Brian who was trying not to laugh about the whole thing and waving me on to keep walking in line. I picked up my bucket and walked on.

Around six in the evening it was too late to keep moving and the scrap metal was weighed. The marine team had surpassed the army and would just fuel the competition for the next day. The army and marine teams would out do each other over and over as the two weeks went by.

As I climbed up the truck to head back for dinner, I looked at the field I had crossed and "cleared" for civilian contractors. There were dozens of little red flags waving in the hot Kahoolawe wind throughout the field I had walked on. Bombs and other ordinance that failed to explode when they were dropped by jets or fired from ships at the target areas over the last few decades.

Dinner was followed by ice cream and even a movie played on a VCR and television set. The EOD tried to make it a comfortable as possible in order to keep our brains from realizing what the hell we were doing. For two weeks it went on like that. Walk, clear, little red flags, walk, clear and dump our buckets of scraps. Well, the ice cream was decent. I had some every night, I will tell you now, I never missed a bowl. I figured if it might be the last.

The weekend that separated the two weeks of work was free time and most of the soldiers headed to the small bay and beach area about a mile from the huts. Brian and I took one of the old military jeeps and loaded it up with fuel, water and food. We took off to see the island of Kahoolawe. The EOD guys said to just be back before night fall as it gets pitch black and there really were not any "safe" places to be for the night except the huts.

The trip around the island was great. Small fishing huts were built by poachers who no doubt snuck over to the island illegally to fish the untouched waters. There were two or three abandoned homes on Kahoolawe that may have been there from before the military took it over. Baxter and I also found huge unexploded bombs just laying in the sand. We stopped to take some pictures with them as we knew no one would believe the images of 1000+ pound bombs that seemed to just be tossed like toys over the sand.

When Baxter and I arrived at the far end of the island from the Seabee huts we were amazed at the sights. We could see Maui, Lanai, Molokini and even Molokai. To the East we could see the mountains of the Big Island of Hawaii. Maunaloa and Maunakea. It had to be one of the best views in all of the island chain. No one could see it though. Kahoolawe was off limits.

Brian and I had lunch overlooking this amazing view. I commented that one day this spot would be multi million dollar estates for the super rich and famous trying to escape the urban world of America's big cities. I liked Kahoolawe more the way it was, quiet and pure.

After lunch we took some final pictures and headed back for the base. Kahoolawe did not take Brian's or my life during those two weeks. It's views and simple beauty did, however, take our breath away. I will always remember the craziest mission I ever volunteered for.

Serving up the grub in the Reclaimer's mess decks. The author is seen returning rude comments about his cooking. Enlisted sailors on the Reclaimer could expect at least three months of duty in the mess decks upon arrival to the ship.

The author with the ship's mess specialist Morgan. The cramped galley had to serve four meals a day around the clock for the ship's crew, regardless of heavy sea conditions.

Some of Starkey's boys. Five divers man the lines as the Reclaimer pulls into port. The quarterdeck podium can be seen behind them.

Fishing was not uncommon during outer island trips. Here a nice catch is pulled in by hand by two of the Relciamer's sailors.

Peter and big John stand in the cramped and miserable quarters that housed over twenty divers and deck division sailors. The crew's quarters always had a stale and moldy smell and was seldom cleaned.

Master diver Ed Starkey and his wife Rowie on the Reclaimer during a short cruise that included family members.

The author at battle stations underway during a training exercise. Position is starboard M60 gunner.

Starkey's boys at Sandy Beach, Oahu, Hawaii. One of many Volkswagon vans owned by the divers on board is seen here. Surfing and beach time was a welcome break from the heavy and arduous work conditions on board the ship.

A weekend day underway on the Reclaimer. Games such as ring toss were stress relievers.

Reclaimer divers explore the fresh water caves of Kauai island. The Reclaimer made several trips to the outer islands of Hawaii. Due to the ship's shallow draft it could enter some of the smaller ports on Kauai and Molokai.

Outer island surfing off the rocky coast of Kauai, Hawaii.

Some the Reclaimer's divers set out to explore Seattle, WA, by night.

Exploring the ruins of several pirate forts and castles on the Pacific coast of the nation of Panama.

Hiking the state trails on the island of Molokai.

Our host to the island, the "mad dog of Molokai".

The author posing on Kahoolawe island next to an unexploded bomb large enough to level a city block. Divers were recruited to help round up and detonate unexploded ordinance on Kahoolawe island after decades of bombing practice there.

Dug in deep in Kahoolawe's red dirt and mud.

The author kneels next to a bomb crater on Kahoolawe. The crater pictured was created from the world's largest non-nuclear explosion that was conducted on the island of Kahoolawe after WWII. The explosion broke open the natural water supplies deep in the island and left Kahoolawe lifeless. The crater is hard to size by the picture, but it is the size of a stadium and contains a fresh water lake inside.

A kind parting thought from master chief master diver Ed Starkey, United States Navy, Retired. Hooyah, Master Diver!

Chapter 9
To the ocean's floor and back.

Eventually the Reclaimer crew wore out our welcome in the Pearl Harbor barracks and we were back on board the ship.

I rolled out of the hard steel bunk in the deck department berthing. Monday morning. Half asleep and hung over. It was instinct by now. I did not even have to be coherent to function by the last few months on board the Reclaimer. The noise of thirty other guys waking, bumping into bunks as they pulled on coveralls and steel toe boots, woke me up better than any alarm clock. I peeked out from the dark blue curtain that was pulled across my middle bunk and surveyed the room before I rolled out.

The deck apes pushed their way out of the berthing and into the stainless steel head. The showers and sinks ran for about two hours straight as guys got ready for the day. Some would head to the mess decks first while others showered. It was organized that way, we sort of had our routines. The Reclaimer was home for us. After two years that sunk in and it was not as painful to think about any more.

One of the deck department guys had painted a cartoon ape on the door to the deck berthing. At first the other departments teased us about it, but the picture became an image of pride after a week or so. It was detailed more as the months went on to look even better, I wish I had a photo of it to include in the book as it summed up our departments personality very well. Deck department, including the divers like me who were attached to it, were hard laborers, but we had pride and we were a team.

The morning meant at least four cups of coffee and a full breakfast. I learned to eat well in the navy as I burned calories working in the heat all day on the ship. Painting, grinding, welding or heavy lifting, I burned my meals off. For breakfast I would pile the potatoes, pancakes, rice, eggs and meats high. Each cup of coffee was black and thick. I choked them down every morning with my meal and started my day.

Guys would chat with each other about the night before. The would talk about where they went out to party and drink. For the divers it was usually live music joints like Anna Bananas or the Wave. Basically places that we could fit in which meant the weirdest places we could find. None of us looked military any more. Long hair and two day old shaves, we looked like twenty-something slackers. What made it worse was that about six of us had Volkswagen "bugs" and vans that we caravanned out to the bars in. Each was painted in bizarre and eclectic patterns of color and imagery.

As we got ready for the day we laughed at the stories each would tell. Not even eight a.m. and we were already planning the night out. Someone would have the scoop on a live reggae group playing near the University of Hawaii at Manoa or perhaps a cheap draft beer special in Waikiki. By lunch we would have our plans set.

When we actually drove off the base, winding our way through the streets as a convoy of beat up Volkswagens, we would stop at the military package store on Hickam AFB to buy some beer. I kept a cooler in my van that doubled as a hand rest between the two front seats. My van was my home away from the ship. I had a sleeping bag, two pillows, carpets on the floor and a curtain to close off the driving area windows incase I needed to crash in a parking lot somewhere.

It was a good plan, actually. I never had to drive drunk. I could stumble out of Anna's at about two a.m. and get hours of good sleep in my van before heading back to base. I even learned to set my alarm clock in the van before I went into the establishment as I never knew what condition I would be in coming out.

I was nearing the end of my Reclaimer tour and it gave me hope, a sort of light at the end of a dark tunnel. I was numb to my daily work which included both deck department labor and diving jobs. On a given day I was assigned to repaint…well…just about any damn thing. The saying in the navy was " if it moves, grease it, if it doesn't , paint it." I would make my way to the paint locker every morning and stock up.

Inside the paint locker would be hundreds of gallons of gray, white, black and terracotta red paint. Primers and glues were also thrown about for good measure. Generally a few deck guys would be hung over and sleeping on a pile of paint cans in the locker trying to stay out of the supervisor's eyesight. I would step around them and grab a gallon of whatever I needed and a few brushes that spent the night soaking in thinner.

The fumes of paint and thinner were thick in the paint locker. The guys crashed out inside must have burned a few million brain cells sleeping in there for hours. Not that any change in their personality could be noticed afterwards.

I remembered to grab a handful of rags from the locker as well. The rags came to the ship in hay bail looking loads. The bails of old clothing was probably sold to the navy from Goodwill and the Salvation Army. It was comprised of the clothes that were not fit to sell in their stores around Hawaii. The strange thing was, as I dug through the bail of rags, many of the shorts and shirts compressed into the heap did not look to darn bad to a guy making less than a thousand dollars a month. Many a shirt and jeans ended up in my locker from those rag bails.

I cleaned, chipped, grinded and repainted whatever they assigned me to work on. I knew that the second half of the day I could go down into the dive locker. That was how it worked. Divers spent the morning assigned to deck division and the afternoons in the diving spaces maintaining our recompression chamber and dive gear.

The locker always had work to be done. Mark 12 helmets needed to be dismantled and lubricated so that the ship's air conditioning and Hawaii heat did not destroy the rubber and nylon seals. It would not be good to find a helmet leak when a diver was at two hundred feet and ten yards into a dark sunken ship's interior. I cleaned and repaired the dive gear like I had to dive in it myself the next day.

Diving umbilical cords were handed out to the fantail from the storage spaces below to be inspected and retied. Each cord had three components. One hose for air, one cable for communications and one steel cable for strength and support. The three were kept together with brown twine and had to be retied about every two years.

The diving jobs got better as my two years on board went on. I looked forward to the dive time and the peacefull effect of being underwater. When we were assigned to inspect a sonar beacon off the coast of Oahu, our Reclaimer divers were excited. It would be a serious dive station with Helium Oxygen systems being loaded on board to increase our dive potential.

The Reclaimer was docked right at Mobil Diving and Salvage Unit 1, so it was easy to load up a "fly away" mixed gas system onto our fantail. The Reclaimer already had a recompression chamber and air diving compressors. With the added capability of Helium/Oxygen we could dive to three hundred feet for hours. Divers returning from deep dives could decompress in our on board chamber safely or be treated for a dive emergency.

I loved the action of setting up a mixed gas dive station. Hundreds of feet of hoses and cables needed to be assembled and secured to the ship's aft decks. The large panel of gauges that was used to track gas flow and tank pressures was just to the side of where the dive supervisor would control the dive operations. It would take an additional ten to twenty divers from MDSU1 to run the enhanced dive station and keep fresh divers going in the water.

A diver could not just dive over and over. Deep dive operations "burned" divers as the days went on. The navy dive tables and charts explained that divers needed to be on the surface breathing air for certain time periods between both air and especially helium/O2 dives. This meant master divers and dive officers on the Reclaimer had to keep track of what every diver did and how much time they were underwater.

The years I was on the Reclaimer I was a second class diver and could not dive mixed gas. I would go to mixed gas school after the ship tour in Panama City, Florida. For this reason I was relived to hear that both air dives and gas dives would be performed to get everyone in the water.

The Reclaimer was even more cluttered than usual with the addition of a portable He/O2 system on the fantail. We double checked that everything was secured and pulled out of Pearl Harbor for open ocean. The sonar beacons were set out from the island far enough to give them a depth of almost one hundred feet. Some were even deeper which meant we needed the He/O2 system ready. The idea of a beacon was to send a warning out into the ocean to keep submarines from striking the shallow reefs that surrounded Hawaii's shores. Think of them as light houses for submarines.

Diving on a fixed point meant the Reclaimer had to be anchored from the bow and the stern. This would keep us from spinning in the water and tangling the diver's umbilical. The captain positioned the Reclaimer using the sea charts that showed locations of sonar beacons and the Global Positioning System. Errors due to currents and rough seas would have to be dealt with by the divers themselves.

In these kinds of dive operations, divers were lowered two at a time by the ship's boom on an aluminum platform or "stage". Once on the bottom, it was not uncommon for the divers to have to traverse from the stage to the dive job itself. The idea was to pass through the stage in such a way that the umbilical would go through the stage top and bottom platforms. That way a diver could not get lost. The diver just followed the umbilical back to the stage. The Pacific Ocean around Hawaii was clear enough that this may not have been always needed, but we stuck with dive protocol anyway for training.

The full Mark 12 suit was chosen for the sonar inspection and repair. The suit gave the diver good protection and also, when they worked, communications with topside. The Mark 12 helmet could be used alone, but it was awkward and bobbed around with out the firm mount of the suit. It was good experience to gear up divers in the Mark 12. It took two dive-station divers to help one Mark 12 diver suit up. The suit required lead weights, straps, mounting and sealing the helmet.

I was exited to have a chance at the Mark 12. I seldom dove the suit since dive school. Most of those were training dives. Just bottom drops for qualification. Every once and a while we geared up the full Mark 12 rig. This was a real operation and for a young diver to get chosen to participate was a real thrill.

I geared up with the assistance of two other Reclaimer divers. The MDSU1 divers were working the various station watches and would also have a chance to dive as the day went on. It appeared the Reclaimer was getting first billing for dives as we supplied the transportation and platform. The MDSU1 guys were not complaining as it was the other way around when we were called to their command to help with ship's husbandry work in Pearl Harbor. The MDSU1 guys, then, would dive all day as we got to tend umbilical and work the communications.

Master Diver Starkey was working with the dive officers on plans to repair the beacon, but broke off as the dive supervisor, one of the Reclaimer's first class divers, called out that divers were entering the water. We were Starkey's boys and we were going over the side. Starkey wanted to be on station during the operation. Starkey walked over to myself and yanked at a few of the straps connecting my Mark 12 suit. He gave me a stern, one eyed sort of look as if to say "don't screw this up". I knew the look well and it really meant "good luck".

My dive buddy and I were the first two divers down that day. We were assigned to make initial surveys of the beacon and confirm that we would be able to hook up the ship's lift cable to raise and repair it. Years of growth had most likely covered the steel eye on the beacon where the cable would connect to. I would work to break off the growth and check for obstructions.

I had a few heavy tools tied to a leather bag and the divers working the side secured it to the aluminum dive stage for the drop down. Two divers stood by me as I stood up in the heavy and bulky Mark 12 suits and walked with me as I made my way to the stage. One by one my dive buddy and I were positioned on the stage, facing each other. Our hands held on to the aluminum stage on each side.

The guys working the umbilical made sure that they did not get caught as the stage was raised by the ship's boom. If the umbilical were to get snagged on something attached to the ship's side, a pipe or fitting, it would pull the diver right of the stage. In the mark 12 suit it would cause serious injury or even break the diver's back.

Starkey watched from his favorite perch on the side as we were raised, swung over the ocean and lowered down. The stage broke the water and within a few seconds we were dropping towards the ocean bottom. The coolness of the ocean on the Mark 12 suit felt good.

The first thing I had to do when I dropped into the ocean in the Mark 12 suit was readjust my straps. No matter how tight I thought I pulled them, the almost weightless effects of the ocean bobbed my helmet up so that I had to heave it back down. The criss-crossing straps worked well and I could get a good hold on one at a time while still holding onto the stage.

My next concentration was to clear my ears during the decent. A cylinder inside the helmet with old and disintegrating foam rubber on it was used to push my nose onto tight and blow. The idea was it was just like pinching my nose to clear my ears, but it did not work as well. I generally had to use my top lip on the foam as well to get a good seal, which is pretty sick if I was not the first diver of the day. Tasty.

If my ears did not clear, I had to call out for the platform to hold so I could catch up. If my comms were not working I had to signal my buddy on the stage to call topside for a hold. If both of our freaken comms were busted, I was out of luck. I just dropped and blew out my ears.

I had blown both ears out over the two years of diving on the Reclaimer already. Nothing devastating, just ear squeeze (trauma) that perforated both of my eardrums several times. Now it was not uncommon for my ears to just blow out during the start of the dive. It hurt like hell but I did not have to worry about clearing anymore on the way down. I do not know of any divers who left the salvage navy without injuries somehow related to diving.

As the stage arrived at the bottom with a jerk, I called topside for them to give me a few yards of slack. It allowed the ship to bob a little in the waves above without sending me flying of the stage. I notified the supervisor we were heading out, and made my way for the beacon. The umbilical were passing through the stage, as usual. This made for slow progress as I had to stop and pull more slack as I moved along. Eventually the whole stage tipped over and made it even harder to pull.

Tools in hand I walked with the slow and methodical bounce of an astronaut on the moon towards the fifteen foot structure. Huge fish had made the beacon home. It was a wonderful sight to see two and three foot fish, shining brightly, swirling around the structure. I realized that it must be an attraction for sharks coming to feed on these fish as well. All the more reason to get the job done.

I looked up to the surface, almost a hundred feet above, perhaps more now that I had been walking. The Reclaimer looked small and quite cool from this angle. Two anchor chains ran to the bottom holding the Reclaimer tight. My umbilical made its way down to the stage and out to me. The ocean was clear and gave me visibility far out from my dive site. In the distance I could see a small school of fish drifting along the ocean bottom. The fish looked as if they were large, probably good eating. I tuned back to the beacon and moved on.

When my buddy and I arrived at the beacon I pulled out a crowbar and climbed up towards the steel eye at the top. The beacon was pyramid shaped and held a few large electrical devices. A cable ran power to the structure from the island far away. It appeared skeletal and practical in design.

It was a twenty minute job of breaking off growth to clean up the eye. My dive partner sledge hammered some growth off the bottom of the structure to free it from the ocean floor. The fish, of all sizes and colors, darted around me. It was a maze of color and shapes. I kept looking through the fish and out towards the open ocean to see if a larger visitor may come swimming along.

With the beacon ready to get connected to the ship's cable, my buddy and I returned to the stage. The two of us worked to upright the stage and positioned ourselves back onto it. The return trip was slow with a stop for decompression on the way up. The charts gave us plenty of time to work at the depth we were at, but we paid for it in decompression minutes as we traveled to the surface. The idea, again, was to remove excess nitrogen from the divers blood stream.

At the last few feet before the stage broke the waters surface I took a look down to the bottom of the ocean. The school of fish I had seen earlier were now crossing the area of the beacon and made for a picturesque sight. I would not see the Pacific ocean's bottom again for about a year after this dive. I knew I was on my way to Panama City, Florida for He/O2 school and construction demolition training that would take almost a year to complete.

The stage broke the surface and the stage tenders grabbed it. They heaved on the ropes that held the stage steady and pulled us back onto the Reclaimer's fantail. The time clock was running now. Once the supervisor had divers on deck they had to strip them and get them checked for dive related injuries. Primarily, signs of nitrogen poisoning or the "bends".

My dive partner was just about cleared by the supervisor and Starkey when he looked at one of the other divers on deck and commented that he had a headache. The supervisor and Starkey both caught the comment and started to grill him about the headache. Headaches can be a sign of a nitrogen bubble formed in the brain.

Without a clear answer on weather he had the headache earlier or when it started, Master Diver Starkey called for he and I to both get tossed in the chamber and a basic recompression therapy be performed. The tenders walked us over to the huge aluminum cylinder that was the Reclaimer's hyper-baric chamber and we climbed in. One of the ship's medical/diver staff went with us and we were back on our way down. This time simulated by pressurizing the chamber.

Starkey's idea of sending us both was that if I had a problem later he did not want to bring the chamber back up to get me. It was better to just treat us both. There we sat, three guys in their dive shorts sweating in the high pressure O2 filled chamber. We were subjected to various nervous system checks by the dive/corpsman. Luckily the dive station had time to get two new divers' gear set up and hand out some lunch for the whole station.

The pressure in the chamber caused the temperature to rise and the three of us sat and sweated for about an hour. The first level of chamber therapy was designed for this sort of "just in case" treatment. If further nerve issues became apparent, the therapy could stretch out over three to five hours. We waited out our hour and the chamber came back up. The air inside the cylinder became foggy as the air quickly cooled and the pressure dropped.

I was glad to get cleaned up and back on the dive side. I helped to gear up two more divers and drop them down to rig up the beacon. Within an hour the beacon sat on the Reclaimer's fantail and the technicians were looking it over. It would sit there for the rest of the day as the divers swapped sea stories and threw baited lines over the stern.

This final dive station was a welcome experience for me. I would get orders to Panama City, Florida just a few weeks later. I was ready to move on with my dive training and experience. Panama City was the Mecca of Navy diving technology and training. I would attend first class diver school there and learn dive supervision, medicine and underwater demolition.

When the day actually came to step off the Reclaimer for the last time, the ship's quarterdeck watch announced my departure on the ship's main loudspeaker system, the 1MC. "Electrician's Mate, third class, diver, departing". The departure announcement always gathered a small group of friends to the rails of the ship to say goodbye.

I stepped down the gangway towards the pier and even danced a little shuffle foot on the way. That brought a few laughs from the crew who were watching me leave.   I stepped off the gangway, onto the pier and I was officially separated from the command.

My Volkswagen van was loaded with all my worldly possessions. Which was not much. I had orders and tickets to Florida to leave in a few days. The guys on board would meet up with me later for a celebration and send off party.

I had grown more in the last two years than most young men do in ten. The hard work, dangers and camaraderie built my self confidence and character. The stern hand and calm judgment of Master Diver Ed Starkey had left his impression on me as it had on hundreds of divers who had worked with him over the decades of navy diving experience he had.

I left the Reclaimer with friends having been made that I still contact decades later.   I also left with the attitude and work ethic to get a job done and do it right. This trait has stayed with me and helped me become more successful in life, work and family than I could have ever imagined.

I arrived and departed from the Reclaimer with little in physical possessions or material wealth, but I gained so much in that tough and wild two years. I am still realizing today how valuable it was to me.

Hooyah deep sea!

About the Author

Christopher P. LaVoie grew up a military brat and lived on various bases around the United States during his life until his high school graduation in Philadelphia, PA. Christopher joined the United States Navy and volunteered for the Deep Sea Diver program in 1988. Christopher's navy career included two years on the USS Reclaimer ARS 42 as well as Helium/Oxygen dive school, supervisor training and underwater demolition training in Panama City, FL.

Christopher LaVoie still lives in Honolulu, Hawaii where he dives recreationally. He is married with three children and still serves his country in law enforcement as well as in the war on terrorism worldwide.

This book was possible due to the contributions of several divers who served on board the USS Reclaimer ARS 42 with Christopher LaVoie and he would like to express his appreciation for their input and support in it's writing and publication.

Thank you to all of those deep sea divers who have served with pride and honor in the salvage navy.

Made in the USA
Monee, IL
13 July 2022